Content

Laura Mulvey
Kahlo / Modotti – 40 Years Later

It means much to me to be in Cabaret Voltaire in 2022, where you have resurrected the memory of its revolutionary dadaist beginnings back in 1916. It means much to me, most particularly, to see the small exhibition around Peter Wollen's and my interest in and involvement with Frida Kahlo and Tina Modotti. To bring Kahlo and Modotti to the Cabaret Voltaire would have had a particular resonance for Peter; as a teenager in the late 1950s, he was fascinated by the art and literature of dada and surrealism—a threshold, as it were, into all his later preoccupations and activities around the relation between radical art and radical politics. Or rather, a point of origin that stayed with him throughout his life.

These artefacts are archival documents relating to both the exhibition and the film *Frida Kahlo and Tina Modotti* that date from 1982—forty years ago. There is, obviously, a double history here: our moment, the 1970s and early '80s, and the much earlier moment to which we turned: the 1920s and early '30s. There is also, obviously, a double geography: the UK, where Peter and I were based, and Mexico. I want to begin by describing how we came to feel an intense curiosity about this past, the history, and a distant place, which grew into a certain sense of affinity and then a desire to find a way to give an account of the radical Mexican art of the period (1920s–30s) within our own cultural context (1970s–80s). Our fascination with Kahlo and Modotti was very much rooted in the wider context of the Mexican version of modernism. To explain this further, I will discuss how our work on the two artists fits not only with Peter's and my, but also with our generation's, return to the great days of modernism in the post-World War I period—most particularly during the 1920s. And, of course, that foundational moment in 1916 was an inspiration for so much that happened in those years.

To begin at the beginning, our first encounter with Mexico and its revolutionary art came about by chance. One of Peter's and my closest friends, Jon Halliday (an expert, among other things, on Douglas Sirk[1]), was teaching at the Collegio di México in Mexico City in the late 1970s. Peter, teaching at Columbia University, our nine-year-old son Chad, and I were all in New York when Jon invited us to

---

1   See *Sirk on Sirk: Interviews with Jon Halliday*, London: Secker and Warburg and BFI, 1971; and see also the publication to mark the occasion of the Sirk retrospective at the Edinburgh Film Festival in 1972, Laura Mulvey and Jon Halliday (eds), *Douglas Sirk*, Edinburgh: EFF, 1972.

visit him and his girlfriend, the singer Francine Winham, in Mexico, for Christmas and the New Year in 1978–79. The visit turned out to be an astounding experience for us, and most particularly for Peter.

Peter had been a key figure among art and film historians, critics, and curators who began, during the 1960s, to look back to the artistic avant-gardes of the 1920s and resurrect ideas and images from the French, German, and Soviet avant-garde movements that had been, as it were, "buried" during the intervening decades. He was particularly interested in Soviet experimental art, literature, and politics, in addition to his longstanding interest in dada and surrealism. However, we arrived in Mexico knowing very little, or probably nothing, about its revolutionary art and culture. The Mexican Revolution and its radical art movements hadn't been explored by the British culture of the left (although there were, of course, specialist art historians who were familiar with the history), and Peter was very struck by this lack of awareness on our part. He immediately set about absorbing this extraordinary art, its history and radical implications, its connections to surrealism, as well as the parallels, but also the divergences, between the Soviet and Mexican movements. At that point, we had never heard of either Frida Kahlo or Tina Modotti. Needless to say, alongside our extended visits to, for instance, the murals by Diego Rivera and José Clemente Orozco, we went to Kahlo's Blue House in Coyoacán; we were amazed by her art but also by her environment and her life.

When we returned to the UK, we began to question: what kind of exhibition would make the "Mexican Renaissance" better known within our cultural milieu? And even more importantly, how could we make its energy and ideas seem relevant to our present? Journals such as *Screen* and *New Left Review*, among others, had brought, say, Brecht and Benjamin back into contemporary awareness. New interest in Frida Kahlo was beginning to emerge: Heyden Herrera's major book on her had come out in 1978,[2] soon after Mildred Constantine's biography of Tina Modotti,[3] who quite quickly also became an important focus of interest for us, in 1975.

Gradually, Peter and I realised that a juxtaposition between these two women artists would create a "dialogue" about modernism, politics, women's art, and aesthetics—all issues of great significance for us and our contemporaries, but also bringing to the fore the special significance of the Mexican Revolution and "Renaissance." It was also obvious to us, in addition to their intrinsic interest, that Kahlo and Modotti's work would be viable as an exhibition—we decided

---

2   Hayden Herrera, *Frida Kahlo (1910–1954)*, Chicago: Museum of Contemporary Art, 1978.

3   Mildred Constantine, *Tina Modotti: A Fragile Life*, New York: Paddington Press, 1975.

to approach the Whitechapel Gallery. The Whitechapel Gallery had opened
in 1901 and, having promoted experimental contemporary art across its whole
history, occupied an important place among London's, and indeed, British,
galleries. Mark Francis, the assistant director at the time, was interested and
encouraging and took it on with Nicholas Serota's support. From then until
the exhibition opened in 1982, the gallery and Mark Francis gave the project
unwavering support.

*

The Whitechapel Gallery's commitment was not only of crucial importance,
practically and aesthetically, but also represents something very significant
about the spirit of those times. Peter and I had no curating experience; our
knowledge of the subject was not deep and certainly not academic. We were
not, in any way, professionals—perhaps we belonged to the disappearing
world of the dilettante (if this does not sound too self-romanticizing). However,
we were very aware of our own "historical" context, which had significance
beyond us as individuals. It is useful to frame this by providing some background
to the United Kingdom at the time: the concentration of critical and creative
activity in the 1970s constituted an informal "movement," and, typically of such
moments in which ideas and art come together, it manifested itself in an
amalgam of very different kinds of cultural engagements. For instance, alongside
an avalanche of writing about new avant-garde film, there was, as I mentioned
before, new research into the historic avant-gardes of the 1920s that appeared
in a proliferation of small, specialized, theoretical, left-orientated magazines
and journals. This distinct change in direction during the decade, a turn towards
the political and experimental, stands, to my mind at least, as a kind of "flowering,"
as it were, an unconscious celebration of the last few moments before the
onset of Thatcherism and neoliberalism in 1979. And institutions were prepared
to take risks and to value interesting ideas over professional experience, which
brought a kind of informality and casualness to the passions and enthusiasms of
the experimental period we experienced at that time. By the early 1980s, that
particular alliance between grant-giving bodies and the radical art milieu was
taking its last gasps. With the Conservative Party victory in 1979, Margaret
Thatcher had become prime minister and brought the ethos of "value for money"
to government support for the arts, gesturing, no doubt, to the careless and
irresponsible investment in the clearly commercially valueless avant-garde in
the '70s.

Contingency and history: although we were quick to see that our idea had
relevance for our intellectual and political environment, questions multiplied.
How do we transform our idea into an exhibition that would reflect the
intricacies of the Mexican historical and artistic context? How do we focus
on these unknown, but astoundingly interesting, women artists? And con-
ceptually, how do we ensure the project's relevance and make sure that it
"speaks to" that particular moment? To reiterate, from this perspective, we
were not isolated individuals (or an isolated couple), but part of a "moment."
Not an organized or formal movement, but sharing mutually recognized and
collective concerns, summed up by Annette Michelson as "radical aspiration."
Looking back in 2022 to that time, I think it was this moment that made it
possible for us, as I mentioned earlier, to propose the exhibition to the
Whitechapel Gallery without a second thought and for Mark Francis to accept
it in a very similar spirit.

To give a more detailed insight into our deliberations, I have selected a few
symptomatic thoughts and reflections from the exhibition's catalogue:

"Andre Breton went to Mexico, as to a dreamland, to find there that magic
'point of intersection between the political and the artistic lines beyond
which we hope that they may unite in a single revolutionary consciousness
while still preserving intact the identities of the separate motivating forces
that run through them.' (Breton). … Breton's hope, the dialectical unity of art and
revolution, is one that has haunted the modern period. The fact that it is still
no more than a hope for us today demonstrates that none of the solutions sought,
by Breton or by others of different tendencies, succeeded with any degree
of permanence. The initial elan at the moment of intersection has not persisted
or been generalized. We are left with a series of talismans, clustered most
often at certain places and certain periods—Soviet art of the immediate post-
revolutionary years, Berlin dadaism, French surrealism, the Mexico renaissance—to which we may turn back for encouragement and understanding. …
Why Mexico? An exhibition of work by Frida Kahlo and Tina Modotti auto-
matically invites questions about 'marginality'—the status, in terms of mainstream
art history as presented in books and museum displays, assigned to Mexican
art and to women's art and (in Modotti's case) to photography. The centres of art
history are in Europe and the United States; Paris and New York are the last
links in a chain which reaches back through Rome and Florence to the classical
civilizations of antiquity. Breaks and diversions are to be smoothed over or
bracketed off, the 'heterogeneous' to be admitted only as an influence. In this

way the originality, scope and richness of Mexican art have been overlooked
or underestimated."[4]

"The second issue of marginality posed by this exhibition is that of women's art.
At this point, the focus of attention shifts away from the actual historical context
in Mexico that influenced Tina Modotti and Frida Kahlo and moves towards the
debates which have developed around feminist aesthetics. It is here that the
importance of the juxtaposition between the two artists comes into relief. An
exhibition of either artist alone would have asserted her individual importance,
her specific contribution to an artistic practice (painting or photography) and
to women's cultural traditions. But the decision to bring the work of Frida Kahlo
and Tina Modotti together is based on something more than the fact that they
have been unjustly neglected and that their art and their lives are of great intrinsic
interest. The juxtaposition is designed to raise a series of aesthetic questions
relevant to feminist aesthetics. ... Secondly, there is the confrontation of the
questions of value posed by the split between high art and applied arts and the
examination of the rationale behind the unbridgeable gap that seems to divide
them. In the present context this last point doubles with the discovery of popular
traditions of Mexican art during this period (the background to Kahlo's work)
and with an avant-garde desire to bring art into dialogue with the modern world
and its technology (a contributing factor to Modotti's use of photography as
political reportage)."[5]

From a theoretical perspective, the exhibition *Frida Kahlo and Tina Modotti*
addressed certain key questions associated with women and art that were being
articulated at the time for the first time. Perhaps the most relevant were: first
of all, challenges to traditional male dominance in the arts, to the aesthetics of
high art as well as the concept of the male "genius"; and secondly, an "archaeo-
logical" search for the lost work of women artists, the rediscovery of their forgotten
histories. This is a moment marked by Sheila Rowbotham in her book *Woman's
Consciousness, Man's World*, published in 1973, where she writes: "The oppressed
without hope are mysteriously quiet. When the conception of change is beyond
the limits of the possible, there are no words to articulate discontent, so it is
sometimes held not to exist. This mistaken belief arises because we can only
grasp silence in the moment in which it is breaking."[6] And this period sees
the beginning of the breaking of ancient silences. Another book by Rowbotham

---

4   The essay from the catalogue has been reprinted in Laura Mulvey, *Visual and Other
    Pleasures,* Basingstoke: Palgrave, 1989, pp. 81–107; here pp. 81–82.
5   Ibid., pp. 83–84.
6   Sheila Rowbotham, *Woman's Consciousness, Man's World,* London: Pelican, 1973, p. 29.

makes it clear: *Hidden from History: 300 Years of Women's Oppression and the Fight Against It* (also published in 1973).[7] Linda Nochlin inaugurated the feminist work of rediscovering lost and forgotten women artists with her essay "Why Have There Been No Great Women Artists?" first published in *ARTnews* in 1971 and frequently reprinted across the decades.[8] She pointed out that the search into the past could not simply be a matter of discovery and enumeration but of research into the historical conditions, socio-economics, and so on, that had excluded women from the elite world of male creativity. It was important to understand that if and when some women artists managed to semi-penetrate that world, it then quickly forgot them. Nochlin's influential essay led to the 1976 exhibition *Women Artists 1550–1950*, which traveled across the United States and literally put the issue on the map—Frida Kahlo was among the eighty-three artists in the show. In 1979, three years prior to our exhibition, Peter had already sensed that the marginalization of women—not only of Kahlo and Modotti— also reflected other forms of limitations: "Most discussion of the avant-garde is both Eurocentric (or North Americanocentric) and male-centric. So that two women artists living and working in Mexico can give a different perspective."[9] I should also mention that the spirit behind these projects inspired similar research into women filmmakers that led to festivals of rediscovered work. My involvement with the 1972 Edinburgh Film Festival's women's event is just one example.[10]

In the UK, the question of lost women artists was pursued by Rozsika Parker and Griselda Pollock in their book *Old Mistresses: Women, Art and Ideology* (1981) as well as by Germaine Greer in *The Obstacle Race: The Fortunes of Women Painters and Their Work* (1979). Also, in 1973, Ursula Owen and Carmen Callil founded Virago Press, and it quickly became an important publishing channel for the feminist movement. About their motivation, Owen has said, "Silences. Perhaps the most important issue addressed in our early publications was the absence of women's voices and experiences in the culture. We wanted to publish books about lives that had been invisible and with sentiments that had been unthinkable."

---

7   See Sheila Rowbotham, *Hidden from History: 300 Years of Women's Oppression and the Fight Against It*, London: Pluto Press, 1973.

8   See Linda Nochlin, "Why Have There Been No Great Women Artists?," *ARTnews*, January 1971, pp. 22–39, here pp. 67–71.

9   Peter Wollen, "Mexico / Women / Art," first published in Emma Tennant (ed.), *Saturday Night Reader,* London: W. H. Allen, 1979, reprinted in Wollen, *Readings and Writings: Semiotic Counter Strategies,* London: Verso, 1982, pp. 105–22; here p. 110.

10 See the dossier on the Edinburgh Film Festival of 1972, in Heide Schlüpmann and Andrea Haller (eds), *Zu Wort kommen / Speaking Up. Remake. Frankfurter Frauen Film Tage / Frankfurt Women's Film Days 2018. A Publication*, Frankfurt am Main: Kinothek Asta Nielsen e.V., 2018, pp. 180–98.

All these initiatives formed the backdrop for our thoughts about the exhibition
and its planning.

*

Peter and I wrote the catalogue essay together, taking responsibility for different
sections but not identifying authorship in the text. It's clear to me now, looking
back, that the contrast between the two artists increasingly began to capture our
collective imagination and interest. The exhibition's organization was reason-
ably smooth. In Frida Kahlo's case, the collectors who owned the artworks were,
at that point in time, before her later rise to extraordinary eminence, prepared
to lend; it also helped that the Whitechapel Gallery was a small but prestigious
institution. In Tina Modotti's case, her photographs all came from the Fondazione
Modotti in Udine, her hometown. The Fondazione had been set up under
the auspices of Vittorio Vidali, a Communist Party activist and Tina's last lover.

However, we had one near-disaster: Dolores Olmedo, a very wealthy and
powerful art collector in Mexico City, was a collector of work by Diego Rivera and
also Frida Kahlo—she had known both artists personally. For the feminist
politics of the exhibition, the paintings that I thought of as the "abject Kahlos,"
which had particular importance and significance, were in Dolores Olmedo's
collection. These are paintings depicting, viscerally and boldly, the female body
as a site of suffering, exposed flesh, bleeding from birth, abortion, and male
violence. While Kahlo's self-portraits display a kind of mask-like surface exteriority,
the "abject paintings" make painfully clear the hidden and unspeakable, that is,
the repressed, concealed behind this enigmatic beauty. Peter and Mark Francis
felt that it was important to meet Dolores Olmedo and make sure that these
specific paintings would be available. Peter, therefore, while in Mexico preparing
for the exhibition, went to her mansion in Mexico City to visit her. It was there
that she announced, "I just bought a very expensive work by Diego Rivera at
Sotheby's in New York. To pay for it, I had to pawn the Kahlo paintings." These
particular paintings were at the pawnbrokers in Mexico, and the ticket was
with Sotheby's. I'm afraid I cannot remember how this was resolved, but it was—
to our great relief—and we did have the "abject paintings" in our exhibition.

*

Now let's turn to the film. We had always intended to make a film arising from
the exhibition. However, there was a time lag between the end of the exhibition
and making the film, during which our ideas became considerably more
streamlined and the dialogue between the two artists became more pronounced,

ultimately structuring the shape and pattern of the film. To put the transition
clearly: the exhibition had, quite obviously, consisted of Kahlo's paintings and
Modotti's photographs on the gallery walls. In the accompanying catalogue
essay, we explained our interest in the two women's lives and their politics,
their attitudes towards the female body, and the significant, but very different,
questions they raise about women's art and aesthetics. Necessarily and obviously,
the ideas and images occupied different spaces. However, on the screen,
it was possible to weave these ideas into a different kind of texture: words could
be juxtaposed with the relevant works, and the various themes could be sys-
tematically arranged into a "dialogic" pattern.

The film was funded by the Arts Council of Great Britain (ACGB), which tradi-
tionally had financed documentary films about art and artists for public screen-
ings primarily in educational spaces such as major museums and art galleries.
The Tate Gallery, Britain's leading museum of modern art at this time, could not,
by order of some decree, include any reproducible images in its collection—
no photographs, no work by artist filmmakers.[11] During the 1970s, drawing on the
experimental work of the UK film movement that I evoked earlier, the ACGB
began to blur boundaries, commissioning experimental filmmakers to produce
what were still documentaries about art and artists, but ones that would deviate
from the earlier, strictly conventional educational formats. Out of this dual situation,
Frida Kahlo and Tina Modotti assumed a dual aesthetic strategy. At first, we had
hoped that meaning, appropriate for the documentary purpose of the commission,
would entirely emerge out of the montaged images.

However, ultimately, the educational remit prevailed; we added a voice-over
text, mostly taken from the essay in the exhibition catalogue, to make the film's
meanings and the artists' stories much clearer and easier for audiences unaccus-
tomed to experimental film to understand. I still feel ambivalent about this
decision. On the other hand, we rejected the use of camera movement over the
artwork, refusing the—perhaps tempting—use of the film and art relationship
to discover and dwell on details. Behind this decision is Peter's and my commitment to symmetry and pattern in all our films. For both of us, symmetry had

---

11 On the Tate Gallery's policy not to collect reproducible works: "Compared with its
    international counterparts, such as the Centre Pompidou in Paris or the Museum
    of Modern Art in New York, both of which hold significant collections of photographs,
    Tate had prevaricated for years over whether photography should be part of its remit.
    Only with the opening of Tate Modern in 2000 did dedicated photography exhibitions
    finally appear on the programme, selected at first by outside curators and adapted
    from exhibitions originated abroad." See the Interview with Simon Baker, The Tate
    Gallery's first curator of photography, appointed 2010, in the *Financial Times*, 15 May 2015.

an aesthetic, modernist attraction. In *Tina Modotti and Frida Kahlo*, pattern dominates and wends its way across the film. Each organizing topic loops back to a joint point of departure: the title page that Julian Rothenstein designed for each chapter. The two artists are juxtaposed within their shared context, the art and politics of post-revolutionary Mexico, but contrasted by a binary structure of oppositions.

On the screen, the images, stories, and ideas that have hovered in the gallery space could come together, fusing into a series of visual juxtapositions and creating a much more vivid dialogue between the two artists. Although our previous films had all been constructed around systems of montage (primarily due to the place of pattern and tableaux in their structure), juxtaposition, in both form and content, was crucial for *Frida Kahlo and Tina Modotti*. The montage opens up a space for a "third meaning," a resonant evocation, through Kahlo and Modotti individually, of women's lives, their struggles, and the particularity of their art more generally.

The Kahlo paintings and Modotti photographs are grouped thematically into three chapters, with two intervening sections focused on the life and image of each of the artists: "Roots/Movement," "Biography," "Inside/Outside," "The Body," "Injury/Beauty." All the chapters set up a contrast between Kahlo's persistent return to painting self-portraits and Modotti's engagement with public spaces. In retrospect, this binary structure seems rather reductive.[12] However, I remember, although neither appear in the film itself, that Eisenstein and montage were very much in our minds as we developed the film, that is, in terms of his film theory and also his relation to Mexico. The sections "Biography" and "The Body" deal with Kahlo and Modotti's lives. As it was so important for the film to put their artwork in the context of their experiences, which was relegated to the catalogue essay for the exhibition, I'll give a brief biographical account of each in this concluding section of my presentation.

To evoke the comparative seclusion of Kahlo's life, the camera roams around the Blue House, which is where she was born and lived until her death; the voice-over mentions the childhood accident that left her struggling with pain for the rest of her life and thus, necessarily, with an acute consciousness of

---

12 It would be wrong to think of Frida Kahlo as permanently cloistered or secluded, despite the injuries that inhibited her physically and her intense attachment to her native home and land. In some ways, it would be easily possible to exaggerate the "rootedness" of Kahlo. In fact, she traveled extensively in the United States, first with Rivera, then on her own account when she was recognized as a painter in her own right, and also for medical reasons. She visited Europe after André Breton returned to Paris full of enthusiasm for her work.

her body. We associated this contingency with some of the recurring themes of her art, in which she took herself as the main subject matter. Her paintings also form a material manifestation of her interior experiences, dreams, and fantasies and seem to act as a "decoration" of and for her life and relationships in a manner similar to the way she decorated herself and her house with the colors and objects of Mexican folk art.

The Tina Modotti section shows a series of maps and traces the journeys that marked her life: born in Italy, she emigrated with her family to the US, moved from San Francisco to Los Angeles, and then from California to Mexico. Expelled from Mexico for political reasons, she arrived in Europe via Rotterdam and then sought political asylum in Berlin until, due to the deteriorating political situation, she took refuge in Moscow. As an agent for the Comintern, she was sent to Paris, then to Spain, and back again to France after the defeat of the Republic by Franco and the fascist forces in the Spanish Civil War. Finally, she returned to Mexico, where she died in 1942 age forty-five.

Modotti did not decorate the places she lived in. As Manuel Alvarez Bravo recalled, "The walls of her studio were white and clean. Later she started to write some of Lenin's and Marx's phrases on them."[13] The ten years or so that she spent in Mexico (the first visit in 1922; the second more or less settled stay from 1923 to 1930; and the final exile from April 1939 until her death) was the longest period spent in a single country during her adult life. It was also the period when almost all her work as a photographer was done.

After her expulsion from Mexico, the ship on which Tina Modotti was deported docked in New Orleans, and she was detained for eight days in the immigration station there. She wrote to Weston:

"[T]he newspapers have followed me, and at times preceded me, with wolf-like greediness—here in the U.S. everything is seen from the 'beauty' angle— a daily here spoke of my trip and referred to me as 'a woman of striking beauty' —other reporters to whom I refused an interview tried to convince me by saying they would just speak of 'how pretty I was'—to which I answered that I could not possibly see what 'prettiness' had to do with the revolutionary movement nor with the expulsion of Communists—evidently women here are measured by a motion picture standard."[14]

The choices that Frida Kahlo and Tina Modotti made, consciously or unconsciously, were clearly linked to their own conditions of existence, class, sex, history, or even chance, showing up the contingent aspects of an artist's work

---

13 Manuel Alvarez Bravo, quoted from Constantine, *Tina Modotti: A Fragile Life.*
14 Letter from Tina Modotti to Edward Weston, quoted from ibid., p. 175.

that can so easily disappear under a cloud of genius. To reiterate and conclude, this conjuncture between history and contingency—how the two artists' work was affected by both the overarching context and the events of their lives— emerged as an important consideration for Peter and me when we were writing the essay for the exhibition catalogue. It had been unfashionable for some time to write about art and artists from a biographical perspective, but in the case of women, their achievements, and their public presence, it seemed impossible, politically and aesthetically, to ignore their personal and individual experiences. In the film, we were able to bring these complicated interactions more to the fore: Frida Kahlo and Tina Modotti's life stories constitute an essential layer in the overall structure of the film and inflect the oppositions that link and interweave with the other sections. In bringing these two women artists together on the walls of the Whitechapel Gallery, in the catalogue essay, and in the film, Peter and I hoped to celebrate their art, their achievements, and the context of the Mexican avant-garde. But we also hoped to articulate and make visible a feminist principle: what Kahlo and Modotti wanted to do and what was possible for them to do, their desires and limitations, were defined by the fact that they were women.

A version of this text was presented by Laura Mulvey at Cabaret Voltaire, Zurich, on November 8, 2022.

Peter Wollen
Fridamania

The first retrospective of Frida Kahlo's work outside Mexico opened at the
Whitechapel Gallery in London in May 1982, organized and co-curated by
Laura Mulvey and myself. In fact, it was a joint exhibition of works by
Kahlo and Tina Modotti, the Italian–American–Mexican photographer, who
herself subsequently became the object of a minor kind of "Tinamania."
At that time, Mulvey and I were hostile to the idea of shows limited to the
work of a single artist and felt that a contrast between two related
bodies of work was more revealing than a self-contained one-person event.
We also wanted to display photography on an equal footing with painting. After its opening at the Whitechapel, the show traveled to Germany
and Stockholm before going on to the Grey Art Gallery in New York and,
finally, to the National Art Museum in Mexico City. The North American
venues were added after the exhibition had opened, as a direct result
of its impact in Europe and its word-of-mouth reputation. The effect of
this was to introduce Kahlo's work to the US—more specifically to its
artistic and intellectual capital, New York—in 1983, at roughly the same
time that Hayden Herrera's biography of Kahlo came out. It was, I believe, the conjunction of these two events, the exhibition and the book, that
sparked off an interest in the US, which later fed into or converged
with the enthusiasm in Europe and Mexico to produce "Fridamania":
the elevation of Kahlo to cult status.

Since then, there has been a stream of further exhibitions, catalogues,
books—and eventually postcards, calendars, wall-posters, folding
screens, diaries, and feature films: Paul Leduc's and now Julie Taymor's.
Within a decade, Frida Kahlo had become probably one of the most
instantly recognizable artists in the world. How did it happen? And why?
As we shall see, these questions raise a number of issues that are central
to the way we construe the history of taste, the reception of art, and
a generation of cultural icons.

In Coyoacán

To begin with the question of why we wanted to put on the show in the first
place: this may verge on self-portraiture, but perhaps that is appropriate

in writing about an artist like Kahlo. We were not art historians and had
never organized an art exhibition before. We were film theorists and
avant-garde filmmakers. We went to Mexico together for a Christmas
holiday in 1978–79, staying with a friend who taught Japanese Political
History at the Colegio de México. Before that, I had seen one Kahlo
painting, *Portrait of Frida and Diego,* at the historic exhibition *Women
Artists: 1550–1950,* put on by Ann Sutherland Harris and Linda Nochlin
in 1976. However, Kahlo did not figure at all prominently in my thinking
as I planned what to see on the trip. There was scant information in the
books I looked at—Rivera's wife, did some painting. I first became more
conscious of her role after arriving in Mexico City, because she is por-
trayed—alongside Modotti—as a revolutionary, handing out arms to the
workers and peasants in the murals Rivera painted in the courtyard of
the Ministry of Education building in Mexico City. Later, we went to the
suburb of Coyoacán, primarily to visit Trotsky's house. The Blue House,
which belonged to Kahlo, was nearby, and so we decided to visit that too.
As it turned out, it was the Blue House that made the greater impact.

In fact, there was only one room of Kahlo paintings there—by no means
the best ones. The impact came from the house itself. Looking back
on it, I located it in my mind in a series that included the Gaudí houses
in Barcelona (especially the Casa Batlló and the roof of the Pedrera)
and the Watts Towers in Los Angeles. I had already, in a sense, "exhibited"
Gaudí via the script of Antonioni's film, *The Passenger,* which I co-wrote
with Mark Peploe some years previously. A number of scenes in the film
are set in Gaudí buildings. In general, I was interested in a certain kind
of intensely personal or "outsider" architecture. I still am. This interest
derives from surrealism, and it came as no surprise that it was André
Breton who "discovered" Kahlo as a painter, wrote the catalogue essay for
her first New York show (1939, at the Julien Levy Gallery), and organized
an exhibition of her work in Paris that same year. Breton personally
instigated the reception of her work abroad, and it was as a surrealist
(or para-surrealist) that she was originally perceived outside Mexico—
and to some extent inside as well.

The "outsider" aspect of the Blue House had another important quality,
beyond its relationship with surrealism. It stood in stark contrast to
the white walls, empty spaces, and techno-hygienic aspects of the typical
museum of modern art. It was a cluttered, domestic space, brightly
colored, and full of idiosyncratic objects. In many ways, I saw Kahlo as
challenging the orthodox doctrines of modernism. First, of course, she

was a woman artist, and, by then, it was already well established that
women had been relegated to a secondary place within the history
of modernism. Second, she was, in a sense, an "outsider" artist, untrained,
non-professional, painting out of her own desire without seeking to ex-
hibit; and this too put her in a marginal position vis-à-vis the mainstream
art world. Third, she was from Mexico, a country outside the European–
United States bloc that was culturally hegemonic. Fourth, she had ties with
surrealism, which, although accepted within the history of modernism,
was still somewhat suspect, both within the rationalist Bauhaus account
of art history and within the Greenberg art-for-art's sake version. I was
also interested in the implications of her political involvements—with
Trotsky but also with orthodox Communism.

After visiting the Blue House, I made more of a conscious effort to see
Kahlo's work, and the decisive moment probably came when, shortly
afterwards, I saw the paintings exhibited in the Modern Art Museum in
Chapultepec Park, especially *The Two Fridas*, certainly her most ambi-
tious work available to me. On returning to London, we went to the
Whitechapel Gallery and suggested an exhibition—a project accepted
by the director and by Mark Francis, the in-house curator responsible.
I made a number of trips to Mexico, by myself and then with Mark Francis,
to trace all the work and secure the loans. During this time, I met Hayden
Herrera through mutual friends; we were able to exchange information—
although I learned more from her than she did from me. Her work was
already more advanced than mine, although the book finally appeared
after the show. During this time, I also wrote a piece, a hybrid of fiction
and essay called "Mexico/Women/Art," which was published in London
in 1979 in the *Saturday Night Reader*, an anthology edited by Emma Tennant.

I recently reread this piece for the first time in many years and was
intrigued to see the line I took. The first paragraph mentions Rivera and
muralism, Breton and surrealism, Trotsky and revolutionary communism.
But its centrepiece is "her unrelenting struggle against injury and ill-health."
As we shall see, this was a crucial element in the construction of the
Kahlo legend. I go on to stress the "non-Western" (or "Third World") aspects
of Kahlo's art and compare Mexico with Iran, a country in which I had
lived for some time. I was clearly preoccupied with questions about the
history of modernism and the meaning of the idea of an "avant-garde,"
issues that simultaneously arose for me out of my work as a filmmaker.
I was also fascinated by Kahlo's use of popular art and imagery, especially
the ex-voto paintings she collected, which relate directly to her own

history of medical disasters. I was interested in the ways in which the
avant-garde of the 1960s — Fluxus, for example — picked up the threads
of the 1920s — women's art, political art, photography, popular imagery,
environment, performance — and how these threads were also relevant to
Kahlo. There is a whole section on Kahlo's use of Tehuana costume, linking
it to feminism, to the tragic drama of the body, to the "creolization"
of Indigenous cultures, and to the psychoanalytic theory of masquerade.

Cult Formation

In a way, I was trying, through a consideration of Kahlo, to develop a theory
of what was not yet called postmodernism, through recourse to the repressed other side of modernism, while retaining the very non-postmodern
concept of the avant-garde. In a way, I saw Kahlo as presaging a different
kind of avant-gardism, as a proleptic art-historical mutation. The things
that interested me in her work were in many ways the same things that
drove the formation of the Kahlo cult. The work had immediate relevance
and a powerful impact for me personally back when I first encountered
it; so, in a certain sense, I should not have been so surprised when, as the
work became disseminated, it began to have such a powerful effect on
others. This is all the more true, perhaps, in that I was not an art historian
or a museum professional. I was myself a lay viewer. Yet the formation
of a cult requires more than personal relevance or impact, however powerful, and I believe Fridamania is a kind of cult, seeming, at times, like
the classic cult of the Virgin of Guadalupe (or the Mater Dolorosa) in its
implications and intensity. Kahlo, too, has her disciples, her devotees,
her pilgrims, and even her altars. There have to be specific features in the
work that converge towards the generation of a cult, but there also has
to be something else — a relationship between work and life, a certain
historical context. What follows are some hypothetical suggestions about
cult formation and its preconditions.

First, there was the rise of feminism and the associated interest in
women's art. Kahlo's work was originally (partially) introduced into the
United States in a Chicano context, on the West Coast, a few years before
the Grey Art Gallery show. But it was as a woman painter that she seized
the public imagination. In many ways, she was an ideal candidate for
culthood. She was dead, and therefore monumental in a way barred to any
living artist without being too remote in time. She died in 1954, still in

her early forties. She was also Mexican—in a way that enabled her to appear both as a "Third World" artist, even a woman of color, and as an artist who was herself able to appropriate the "otherness" of Mexico to double the primary "otherness" of being a woman. She was overshadowed by a more famous husband—as were Sophie Taeuber, Sonia Delaunay, Varvara Stepanova, Gabriele Münter, Barbara Hepworth, Georgia O'Keeffe, Lee Krasner, and others. Her situation was both typical in this crucial respect and untypical in others. She was a deeply wounded woman, literally—if also psychologically, by aspects of her relationship with Rivera. The mystique of the suffering artist has always been powerful, but its effect was intensified in the context of feminism.

Second, the rediscovery of Kahlo coincided with the return of figuration in painting in the 1970s: Kiefer, Immendorf, Chia, Clemente, Salle, Fischl. This was linked, of course, to the decline of high modernism, the backlash against conceptualism, and the rise of the idea of postmodernism. This painting, however, was almost exclusively a male affair. Women artists were on track two—photography, the medium used by Kruger, Sherman, and others. Kahlo suggested an alternative pictorial tradition for women, one that was given added force by her choice of self-portraiture as a primary mode. Her art was intimate, private, and personal; it was about her identity as a woman and as a Mexican; it was about the body—very specifically the female body and, even more specifically, her own; it was about babies or the lack of them, clothes and their signification, the contradictory projection of both strength and weakness. It was in violent contrast to the pretentious asceticism of much late modernism, to its vatic emptiness, to its tedious aspiration to be high art, to its ultra-refined painterliness. Moreover, Kahlo's paintings, though small in size, unlike much male gallery art, were immediately striking, poignant, even violent in their attack. They prevailed, in part, because of their sheer quality. They also reproduced well—and this is meant as a compliment rather than a reproach.

More needs to be said about the cult of the "suffering artist"—a phenomenon that underlies earlier cults such as those of Van Gogh, Modigliani, and even Judy Garland or Marilyn Monroe. The "suffering woman artist" brought with it an extra emotional charge—personal suffering was overlaid on gender victimization in a way that facilitated intense psychological identification with the cult figure. Kahlo's art, of course, is much more complex than this formulation suggests, but cults are not themselves driven by a concern with complexity. In many ways, the closest analogy to the cult of Kahlo is that of Sylvia Plath. Plath, too, was damaged and hospitalized — although psychologically rather than physically — and lived through a deeply ambiguous and painful relationship with a more famous husband. (Of course, degrees of fame change over time. Kahlo may well be more famous now than Rivera, Modotti than Weston. I believe that in both cases, their work now sells for more than that of their male partner.) The energy driving interest in Plath plainly comes from a complex of victimization, blame, abjectness, and a fascination with violence, inwardly and outwardly directed. Much the same could be said about Kahlo.

In both cases, the cult is sustained by the construction of a multiplicity of different types of documentation: the publication of the work, of biographies, collections of letters, private diaries, critical assessments, books of photographs, films, and television programmes, as well as the related works of their husbands or other intimates. This buildup of sources makes possible a much stronger identification than would be possible simply from the work itself. Devotees can feel they know the object of their devotion in a detailed and intimate way, one that provides privileged insights into the idol's emotional life. This is not simply the accumulation of trivia; as more and more material on their private lives is made available, the sense that one can understand how Kahlo or Plath felt, that one can identify with their deepest and innermost feelings, becomes more convincing. In this sense too, the Blue House is also a site with a strong emotional charge, comparable to that provided by Charleston or Virginia Woolf's home, similarly open to the public, in consolidation of the Bloomsbury cult. Culthood relies on this kind of identification. It becomes self-sustaining, as the growth of a cult provides its own audience for more publications that have to be filled with more information, images, and commentary.

Concealment and Display

Of course, the personal material on which Kahlo drew when she painted remains important and significant, not in any way irrelevant to her art. Problems only arise because there is simultaneously a drive towards simplification. In reality, Kahlo's art is unusually complex and contradictory, as indeed is Plath's. We can see this by looking, for example, at the role played by Kahlo's costumes in her self-portraits and, as we know from biographies and photographs, in her self-presentation in everyday life. In the first instance, her choice of traditional Mexican costume, particularly

long skirts, reflects the need (or desire) to conceal her injuries, sustained
in a traffic accident when she was eighteen. An electric train crashed
through the bus on which she was traveling. Kahlo was impaled on a broken
piece of steel handrail from the lead car of the train. Her spine was broken in three places, two ribs were broken, her pelvis was broken in three
places, her collarbone was broken, her right leg had eleven fractures,
her right foot was crushed, and the left shoulder dislocated. Plainly, what
she wore served to conceal the extent of her injuries. The particular
choice of clothes, however, also served to remind viewers of the injuries by
drawing attention to the studied idiosyncrasy of her dress through a kind
of "negative display." Kahlo made her costumes into extreme and multiple
signifiers, and, as time went on, they became increasingly elaborate.

Second, the clothes simply signified her Mexicanness. In the 1920s,
following the Mexican Revolution, this was an unproblematic choice.
Kahlo, however, persisted in this emphasis throughout her life, becoming
more extreme as she adopted Tehuana costume as her preferred style.
It seems that, originally, this may have been to please Rivera, who frequently visited the Isthmus of Tehuantepec and painted the women there.
After his return to Mexico from Paris shortly after the stabilization of
the Revolution, Rivera was sent on a visit to Tehuantepec by his patron,
José Vasconcelos, then Minister of Education. Vasconcelos wanted to
de-Europeanize Rivera, to restore his sense of Mexicanness, and chose
Tehuantapec as the representative site of an unspoiled, yet rich, native
culture. As it happened, the region was most renowned for its women —
both for their social status as "strong women" and for their striking local
costumes. (They were also famed for their unembarrassed nudity. Naked
Tehuanas standing in the river were a frequent subject for folkloric photography.) Rivera learned the lesson Vasconcelos intended and painted
images of Tehuana women in full costume in the Ministry of Education
murals, which he executed after his return. He retained his artistic
interest in the women of the Isthmus and, supposedly, was pleased when
Kahlo adopted their style. In any case, she clearly made it her own.
It combined the imagery of the strong woman, the matriarch, with that of
authentic Mexicanness (at least, according to legend), as well as making
a virtue out of necessity by turning defensive concealment into aggressive
and extravagant display.

Rivera himself was renowned as a mythomane, a compulsive liar, and
inventor of amazing tales. As Kahlo noted, he was a fabulist on a grand
scale rather than a petty deceiver. He was also a fervent publicity seeker

who consciously projected a larger-than-life image. In this respect, Kahlo learned from Rivera how to create a vivid public legend of oneself. The fact that she was intent on creating her own mythic identity—of which the cripple/Tehuana complex was the central element—itself facilitated the creation of a cult many years after her death. Paradoxically, perhaps, her highly semioticized self-presentation only had its full effect at a kind of meta-level, through her self-portraiture, as it appeared to a quite different audience in a context far from any she had anticipated. It is important to stress that Kahlo's self-portraiture was imbricated with self-fabulation from a very early stage. The self she portrays is a constructed and carefully contrived one that finally crystallizes in the imagery of Frida-as-Tehuana, which appropriates what was for her, as for Diego, as indeed for us, an exotic image and develops it for her own purposes.

In the early 1990s, I saw an exhibition in Mexico City on representations of Tehuana women by Mexican painters from the early nineteenth century through to the present. The imagery Kahlo used falls into a long tradition of pictorial representations of the Tehuana and celebrations of tropical and feminine Mexico. This imagery changed as artistic styles did, but also as attitudes to the Isthmus and the South evolved. Different artists used the Tehuana image in very different ways. Saturnino Herrán evokes the Andalusian gypsy; Adolfo Best Maugard assimilates the Tehuana to the Indian houri; Roberto Montenegro's portrait of Rosa Rolando in the elaborate face-encircling Tehuana headdress is severe and makes her look like a Mother Superior. Rivera stresses a haughty aloofness and self-possession, preferring images of men and women together, dancing the sandunga. Tina Modotti (in her photographs) shows women at menial work or with infants and small children; Miguel Covarrubias stylizes and emphasizes Indianness; and so on. More recently, the photography of Graciela Iturbide and the paintings of Julio Galán strike a more eccentric note, garish and even grotesque.

Kahlo uses Tehuana costume explicitly as a form of masquerade with multiple and contradictory associations: masquerade as a signifier of and defence against femininity; of—and against—physical damage and trauma; masquerade as an exaggerated signifier of Mexicanness, concentrated in the legend of the Isthmus. Masquerade, of course, is always, necessarily, in some sense, a theatrical mode. Kahlo dramatizes herself through her costume. On one level, this is the simple display of identification with the other that accompanies all exotic dress, whether hippie street fashion or designer clothes from Zandra Rhodes. At another level, it dramatizes the trauma Frida Kahlo had undergone, with its symbolic implications of rape and castration. These implications, in turn, link the physical maiming to the symbolic maiming we can associate, in psycho-analytic terms, with femininity. At the same time, the fearless exhibitionism and bravura of the costume convey pride and self-confidence. This, in turn, can be associated with the folkloric association of the Tehuana woman with power and strength, with Tehuantapec as the site of a mythical matriarchy. As with Plath's symbolic universe, the central metaphors are used to convey both extreme and contradictory fantasies. In two important paintings, the costume is depicted on a hanger, detached from the body, a signifier in its own right.

Those Eyes

Kahlo's iconography is carefully controlled and contains other significant elements beyond costume. Her hair becomes a metaphor, whether close-cropped or flowing luxuriously, adorned with ribbons, combs, flowers, or butterflies. Some paintings show her moustache; others eradicate it. She tends to emphasize the single, strong, continuous line of her eyebrows, whereas in photographs this striking feature is much less pronounced, even absent. Her self-portraits always have a powerful, directed gaze, looking straight out at the viewer. "Look at those eyes," Picasso supposedly wrote to Rivera, "neither you nor I are capable of anything like it." Apoc-ryphal or not, it seems right to compare Kahlo's concern over eyes in her paintings with Picasso's. They immediately engage the viewer, piercingly, with complete self-possession. Finally, there are the accoutrements—above all, the wounds and the monkeys. The wounds speak for themselves, although where they are most blatantly and bloodily displayed—as in the series that followed her miscarriage in Detroit: *Henry Ford Hospital* and *My Birth*—or displaced, as in *A Few Small Nips* or the ex-voto *The Suicide of Dorothy Hale*—they are directly related to the themes of birth and death as violent acts. The monkeys—mimics, grimacers, pets—are associated with infants (desired, miscarried, defunct), with Diego (as ape, as child), with Frida herself (with facial hair), with Mexico (its exuberant local fauna), and with tropical nature (contrasted with the cold industrial north). Again, the apparent stylistic simplicity of Kahlo's paintings, with their vernacular sources, is belied by its metaphoric and allegorical complexity.

Kahlo's relationship with the imagery of Mexicanness has also played
a part in the reception of her work abroad. Mexico has long had an appeal
for artists and intellectuals, becoming a kind of semimythical country,
a site for the projection of dreams and fantasies: Mayakovsky, Eisenstein,
Lawrence, Lowry, Huston, Hart Crane, Edward Weston, Burroughs,
Breton—the list goes on. Eisenstein in particular internalized the legends
of Mexicanness—including those of Tehuantapec and the sandunga—
and sought to reproject them outside in his film *¡Que viva México!* The
cult of Kahlo draws on this historic fascination, a mythology first constructed in Mexico itself during the "Mexican Renaissance" of the 1920s as
a myth of identity, then refashioned elsewhere or by visitors as a myth
of otherness. This mythology of Mexico is one of an alternative America,
constructed in contrast and opposition to the North, to the United States.
Nature versus manufacture, dream versus reality principle, magic and
miracle versus science and technology, essential humanity versus mecha-
nization, enjoyment versus work or repression, acceptance versus denial
of death. These antinomies also structure Kahlo's work—as well as the uto-
pian vision of the grafting together of the two, which she and Rivera
saw metaphorically realized in the agricultural experiments of Luther
Burbank. The availability of this myth—and its potential attractiveness,
as with all myths of otherness—provides a foundation for Fridamania.

Myth and Monster

From a purist point of view, the cult of Kahlo may seem to disqualify her
from being a great artist. But this is no truer of Kahlo than it is of Plath.
Looking for a moment at literature rather than visual art, it has always
struck me that literary critics are deeply ambivalent about works with
mythic status. Melville's Great White Whale is acceptable, even admirable,
yet Mary Shelley's Frankenstein's monster is less so; Bram Stoker's
Dracula hardly acceptable at all. And what about J. M. Barrie's Peter Pan
or Wodehouse's Jeeves? In art history, these issues hardly come up at all
—mythic iconic figures belong to the movies or to strip cartoons, not to art
at all. Only with pop art, when Lichtenstein or Warhol produce works
parasitic on popular art, is this popular mythology admitted, and then it
is assumed that, as a metadiscourse, high art somehow elevates its subject matter by appropriating it. Myth is somewhat different from cult, but
the two are closely connected. Cult figures almost always draw on myths,

just as cult films do: *Casablanca, Rebel Without a Cause, Blade Runner.*
In the case of Kahlo, the growth of Fridamania is partly dependent on
her manipulation of mythic and psychoanalytic material, but at the same
time, Kahlo's art is unthinkable without it.

Given the cultural status the art world assigns to itself, there could
plainly be a tendency for Kahlo's status as an artist to fall as her status
as a cult figure rises. This is not necessarily the case, as the example of
Van Gogh demonstrates—although Toulouse-Lautrec would probably be
a better comparison here. I believe, however, that as the modernist para-
digm disintegrates, her position as an artist will remain secure. Whether
we look at Kahlo from the vantage point of women's art, "Third World"
art, or surrealism; whether we are interested in the appropriation of vernacular forms or the crossover between outsider and fine art, we will
find Kahlo's paintings staring us right in the face. As a woman artist, Kahlo
is certainly comparable with Tanning, Carrington, Agar, or the more
mainstream female surrealists, all of them underestimated; and as a surrealist *tout court* she is comparable with Miró or Matta or Lam or
Masson. Mexican art is due for revaluation, as is the place of the two major
women artists, Kahlo and María Izquierdo, within it. Kahlo's use of vernacular forms is complex and unique, and a reevaluation of outsider art,
breaking down the artificial barriers erected around specialized forms
like the art of psychotics or naïve art, can only benefit her. Once we recog-
nize that even an artist like Jackson Pollock has an outsider aspect, it
will be hard to hold such status against Kahlo. Indeed, it may well come
to appear as one of her greatest strengths.

Paradoxically, it was precisely Kahlo's success that threatened to do most
damage by diverting attention from women artists of the 1960s and '70s
whose reputation was still not firmly secured—artists as different as Eva
Hesse, Judy Chicago, or Mary Kelly. Kelly in particular is an artist whose
work is autobiographical in ways that are strangely similar to Kahlo's,
though formally completely different, more intellectually demanding, and
lacking Kahlo's immediate eye-catching appeal. It is important to place
Kahlo alongside artists like these, to recontextualize her historically, in
order to reconfigure the history of women's art itself and establish its
foundations more securely. In a similar way, the "Mexican Renaissance"
also needs to be reconfigured. I began by explaining how I became
interested in Kahlo's work precisely because it seemed to me to challenge
what I saw as orthodox interpretations and doctrines of modernism.
Since then, the reconfiguration of modernism itself has been underway

in many different places, involving many different arguments. Frida Kahlo
was as good a place to start as any other. But we still need to extend
and expand our reconsideration of twentieth-century art, looking at every
aspect of modernism that was marginalized and reconceptualizing the
role of women, non-Western, and outsider or eccentric artists. As we do this,
we shall diminish the importance of Fridamania and be able to focus
once again on the complexity, intensity, and startling beauty of her work.

New Left Review 22 (July–August 2003), pp. 119–30.

Editorial Note

This booklet is the result of Laura Mulvey's visit to the Department of Film
Studies at the University of Zurich in November 2022. In addition to an evening
event and a small exhibition display at the Cabaret Voltaire, the program
included a discussion of *Crystal Gazing* (1982) at the Xenix cinema and a workshop for doctoral students. Between events, Mulvey returned to the hotel to
work on a "secret essay." A few weeks later, it turned out to be her text on Chantal
Akerman's *Jeanne Dielman, 23 quai de commerce, Bruxelles* (1975), which
was unveiled by Sight & Sound on December 1 as the surprise winner of the
"Greatest Film of all Times" poll.

The booklet revisits some of the moments of the last 50 years: Mulvey's
canonical essay on "Visual Pleasure," delivered as a lecture in 1973; two films from
1982 – *Frida Kahlo / Tina Modotti* and *Crystal Gazing* – an essay from 2003
describing the phenomenon of "Fridamania" that analyzes the relationship
between femininity, pop, and society in its relation to artistic modernism;
and finally, the canonization of Akerman's film in 2022. How do these dates
speak to us today?

Mulvey's lecture at Cabaret Voltaire follows the mode of retrospection. It reflects
on the historical conditions that elicited her and Peter Wollen's curiosity about
Frida Kahlo and Tina Modotti 40 years earlier and traces the context of their
joint curatorial work. In addition to their academic and cinematic work, it is this
lesser-known side of Mulvey and Wollen that we want to draw attention to
in this issue.

The binary juxtaposition of Kahlo / Modotti, which the film and the exhibition
took as a structural principle in the 1980s, becomes a playful quartet in 2024 –
Mulvey / Wollen / Kahlo / Modotti – which rearranges and updates the diverse work
steps of retrieval, curatorship, exhibition, filmmaking, reception, and reflection.
Not least with the help of Laura Mulvey, who has joined us in this endeavor –
for which we cannot thank her enough.

Pascal Maslon, Volker Pantenburg, Caroline Schöbi, and Linda Waack
for the Harun Farocki Institut
Zurich, February 2024

Imprint

Editors: Pascal Maslon, Volker Pantenburg, Caroline Schöbi, and Linda Waack
Managing Editor: Pascal Maslon
Design: Daniela Burger, buerodb.de; Assistant: Alix Stria
Proofreading: Mandi Gomez
Lithografie: prints-professional, Berlin

Printing: Druckerei Sportflieger, Berlin
Fonts: Neutral BP, Excelsior
Paper: Munken Lynx, Efalin Feinleinen
Print Run: 1000
ISBN 978-3-00-078431-6

Thanks to Antje Ehmann, Anna Faroqhi, Lara Faroqhi
as well as Laura Mulvey, Salome Hohl (Cabaret Voltaire), Oliver Fuke, Nicolas
Helm-Grovas, Andrey Lazarev (Whitechapel Gallery), Rob Lucas (New Left Review)

Image credits:
pp. 2, 14, 15: Cabaret Voltaire, November 8, 2022, © Romain Mader
p. 16: Installation shots Whitechapel Gallery, Frida Kahlo / Tina Modotti,
26 March – 2 May 1982, © Whitechapel Gallery

www.harun-farocki-institut.org
HaFI 021

HaFI 021 was realized with financial support from the Farocki Forum at the
Department of Film Studies at the University of Zurich.

Inhalt

FRIDA KAHLO AND TINA MODOTTI

Laura Mulvey
Kahlo / Modotti – 40 Jahre später

Es bedeutet mir viel, im Jahr 2022 im Cabaret Voltaire zu Gast zu sein, wo man
die Erinnerung an die revolutionären dadaistischen Anfänge im Jahr 1916 wieder-
belebt hat. Besonders viel bedeutet es mir, die kleine Ausstellung über Peter
Wollens und mein Interesse an und unsere Beschäftigung mit Frida Kahlo und
Tina Modotti zu sehen. Kahlo und Modotti ins Cabaret Voltaire zu bringen,
hätte für Peter einen besonderen Wert gehabt. Als Teenager in den späten 1950er
Jahren war er von dadaistischer und surrealistischer Kunst und Literatur fasziniert – das bildete gewissermaßen eine Schwelle zu all seinen späteren Beschäf-
tigungen und Aktivitäten rund um die Beziehung zwischen radikaler Kunst und
radikaler Politik; ein Ausgangspunkt, der ihn sein ganzes Leben lang begleitet hat.
	Bei den ausgestellten Artefakten handelt es sich um Archivdokumente, die
sich sowohl auf die Ausstellung als auch auf den Film *Frida Kahlo and Tina Modotti*
beziehen und aus dem Jahr 1982 stammen – also 40 Jahre zurückliegen.
Darin liegt eine doppelte Geschichte begründet: unsere Zeit, die 1970er und frühen
80er Jahre, und die viel frühere Zeit, der wir uns zuwenden: die 1920er und frühen
30er Jahre. Darin steckt natürlich auch eine doppelte Geografie: das Vereinigte
Königreich, wo Peter und ich lebten, und Mexiko. Ich möchte damit beginnen,
dass bei uns eine große Neugier auf diese vergangene Geschichte und diesen
fernen Ort entstand, die sich hin zu einem Gefühl der Verbundenheit und dann zu
dem Wunsch entwickelte, die radikale mexikanische Kunst jener Zeit (20er / 30er
Jahre) in unserem eigenen kulturellen Kontext (70er / 80er Jahre) darstellen
zu wollen. Unsere Faszination für Kahlo und Modotti war sehr stark im weiteren
Kontext der mexikanischen Version des Modernismus verwurzelt. Ich will zunächst
beschreiben, wie unsere Arbeit an den beiden Künstlerinnen nicht nur mit Peters
und meiner, sondern auch mit der Rückbesinnung unserer Generation auf die
großen Tage des Modernismus in der Zeit nach dem Ersten Weltkrieg – vor allem in
den 1920er Jahren – zusammenhängt. Und natürlich war dieser Gründungs-
moment von 1916 eine Inspiration für so vieles, was in jenen Jahren geschah.
	Beginnen wir am Anfang: Unsere erste Begegnung mit Mexiko und seiner
revolutionären Kunst kam zufällig zustande. Einer von Peters und meinen
engsten Freunden, Jon Halliday (ein Experte, unter anderem, für Douglas Sirk[1]),

---

1	Siehe seine *Sirk on Sirk. Interviews with Jon Halliday*, London: Secker and Warburg [British Film
	Institute] 1971, und die Veröffentlichung anlässlich der Sirk-Retrospektive auf dem Edinburgh
	Film Festival 1972: *Douglas Sirk*, ed. Laura Mulvey und Jon Halliday, Edinburgh: EFF 1972.

unterrichtete Ende der 1970er Jahre am Collegio di Mexico in Mexiko-Stadt.
Peter, der an der Columbia University lehrte, unser neunjähriger Sohn Chad und
ich waren in New York, als Jon uns einlud, ihn und seine Freundin, die Sängerin
Francine Winham, über Weihnachten und Neujahr 1978 / 1979 zu besuchen. Der
Besuch wurde für uns, und vor allem für Peter, zu einer erstaunlichen Erfahrung.

Peter war eine Schlüsselfigur unter den Kunst- und Filmhistoriker*innen,
Kritiker*innen und Kurator*innen, die in den 1960er Jahren begannen, auf die
Avantgarden der 1920er Jahre zurückzublicken und Ideen und Bilder der
französischen, deutschen und sowjetischen Avantgarde-Bewegungen wiederzu-
beleben, die in den dazwischenliegenden Jahrzehnten sozusagen ‚verschüttet‘
worden waren. Zusätzlich zu seinem langjährigen Interesse an Dada und
Surrealismus interessierte er sich besonders für die experimentelle sowjetische
Kunst, Literatur und Politik. Als wir in Mexiko ankamen, wussten wir jedoch
sehr wenig oder wahrscheinlich gar nichts über die revolutionäre Kunst und Kultur
des Landes. Die mexikanische Revolution und ihre radikalen Kunstbewegungen
waren von der britischen Kultur der Linken nicht erforscht worden (obwohl es
natürlich spezialisierte Kunsthistoriker*innen gab, die die Geschichte kannten).
Peter war über diesen Mangel an Bewusstsein unsererseits sehr erstaunt.
Er vertiefte sich sofort in diese außergewöhnliche Kunst, ihre Geschichte und
ihre radikalen Implikationen, ihre Verbindungen zum Surrealismus sowie die
Parallelen und Divergenzen zwischen der sowjetischen und der mexikanischen
Bewegung. Zu diesem Zeitpunkt hatten wir noch nie etwas von Frida Kahlo
oder Tina Modotti gehört. Neben den Wandmalereien von Diego Rivera und José
Clemente Orozco sahen wir uns natürlich auch das Blaue Haus von Kahlo
in Coyoacán an. Wir waren beeindruckt von ihrer Kunst, aber auch von ihrer
Umgebung und ihrem Leben.

Zurück in Großbritannien begannen wir zu überlegen, wie eine Ausstellung
aussehen könnte, die die mexikanische Renaissance in unserem kulturellen
Umfeld bekannter machen würde. Und, noch wichtiger, wie wir die Relevanz
ihrer Energie und ihrer Ideen für unsere Gegenwart aufzeigen könnten.
Zeitschriften wie *Screen, New Left Review* und andere hatten etwa Brecht und
Benjamin wieder ins zeitgenössische Bewusstsein gerufen. Und ein neues
Interesse an Frida Kahlo begann zu erwachen: Heyden Herreras wichtiges Buch
über sie war 1978 erschienen,[2] und 1975 Mildred Constantines Biografie über
Tina Modotti,[3] die recht schnell ein zentraler Bezugspunkt für uns wurde.

---

2   Hayden Herrera: *Frida Kahlo (1910–1954)*, Chicago: Museum of Contemporary Art 1978.
3   Mildred Constantine: *Tina Modotti: A Fragile Life*, New York: Paddington Press 1975.

Allmählich wurde Peter und mir klar, dass eine Gegenüberstellung dieser beiden Künstlerinnen einen ‚Dialog' über die Moderne, Politik, Kunst von Frauen und Ästhetik eröffnen würde – alles Themen, die für uns und unsere Zeitgenoss*innen wichtig waren, aber auch die besondere Bedeutung der mexikanischen Revolution und Renaissance in den Vordergrund rückten. Es schien uns offensichtlich, dass die Werke von Kahlo und Modotti nicht nur für sich genommen interessant waren, sondern sich auch für eine Ausstellung eignen würden. Wir beschlossen, uns an die Whitechapel Gallery zu wenden. Die Whitechapel Gallery war 1901 eröffnet worden und nahm durch die Förderung experimenteller zeitgenössischer Kunst während ihrer gesamten Geschichte einen wichtigen Platz unter den Londoner, wenn nicht den britischen Galerien ein. Mark Francis, der damalige stellvertretende Direktor, war interessiert und ermutigte uns. Mit Unterstützung des Direktors Nicholas Serota übernahm er das Projekt. Von da an bis zur Eröffnung der Ausstellung im Jahr 1982 unterstützten die Galerie und Mark Francis das Projekt uneingeschränkt.

*

Das Engagement der Whitechapel Gallery war nicht nur in praktischer und ästhetischer Hinsicht von entscheidender Bedeutung, sondern gibt Aufschluss über den damaligen Zeitgeist. Peter und ich hatten keine kuratorische Erfahrung; unser Wissen über das Thema war nicht tiefgründig und schon gar nicht akademisch. Wir waren in keiner Weise Profis – vielleicht gehörten wir zu der verschwindenden Welt der Dilettant*innen (wenn das nicht zu romantisch klingt). Dennoch waren wir uns unseres eigenen ‚historischen' Kontextes sehr bewusst, dessen Bedeutung über uns als Individuen hinausging. In diesem Zusammenhang sind einige Hintergrundinformationen über das Vereinigte Königreich zu dieser Zeit hilfreich: Die Dichte kritischer und kreativer Aktivität in den 1970er Jahren hatte zu einer informellen ‚Bewegung' geführt, und wie es für solche Momente typisch ist, in denen Ideen und Kunst zusammenkommen, manifestierte sie sich in einem Amalgam aus sehr unterschiedlichen Formen kulturellen Engagements. Zum Beispiel gab es neben einer Fülle von Schriften über den neuen Avantgardefilm, wie ich bereits erwähnt habe, neue Forschung zu den historischen Avantgarden der 1920er Jahre, die in einer Vielzahl von kleinen, spezialisierten, theoretischen, linksorientierten Magazinen und Zeitschriften erschienen. Der deutliche Richtungswechsel in diesem Jahrzehnt, eine Hinwendung zum Politischen und Experimentellen, stellt zumindest für mich eine Art ‚Blüte' dar, eine unbewusste Feier der letzten Momente vor dem Einsetzen des Thatcherismus und des Neoliberalismus im Jahr 1979. Und die Institutionen

waren bereit, Risiken einzugehen, interessante Ideen über berufliche Erfahrung
zu stellen, was den Leidenschaften und dem Enthusiasmus unserer experimentellen Zeit in den 1970er Jahren eine gewisse Zwanglosigkeit und Gelassenheit
verlieh. In den frühen 1980er Jahren war diese besondere Allianz zwischen
den Fördereinrichtungen und dem radikalen Kunstmilieu am Ende ihrer Kräfte.
Mit dem Wahlsieg der Conservative Party im Jahr 1979 wurde Margaret Thatcher
Premierministerin und brachte das Ethos des ‚Preis-Leistungs-Verhältnisses‘
in die staatliche Kunstförderung ein, was zweifellos eine Geste gegenüber den
leichtfertigen und unverantwortlichen Investitionen der 1970er Jahre in die
kommerziell offensichtlich wertlose Avantgarde war.

*

Kontingenz und Geschichte: Die Bedeutung unserer Idee für unser intellektuelles
und politisches Umfeld erkannten wir schnell. Trotzdem stellten sich viele
Fragen. Wie sollte die Idee in eine Ausstellung umgesetzt werden, die die Beson-
derheiten des historischen und künstlerischen Kontextes in Mexiko widerspiegelt? Wie kann man sich auf diese unbekannten, aber außerordentlich
interessanten Künstlerinnen konzentrieren? Und in konzeptueller Hinsicht:
Wie kann man die Relevanz des Projekts sicherstellen und dafür sorgen, dass es
sein Publikum zu diesem besonderen Zeitpunkt ‚erreicht‘? Wie bereits gesagt:
Aus dieser Perspektive waren wir keine isolierten Einzelpersonen (oder ein
isoliertes Paar), sondern Teil eines ‚Moments‘. Wir waren keine organisierte oder
formelle Bewegung, sondern teilten gegenseitig anerkannte und kollektive
Anliegen, die Annette Michelson als ‚radikale Bestrebungen‘ zusammenfasste.
Aus dem Jahr 2022 zurückblickend denke ich, dass es dieser Moment war,
der es uns ermöglichte, der Whitechapel Gallery die Ausstellung vorzuschlagen,
ohne lange darüber nachzudenken, und dass Mark Francis sie aus einer
ähnlichen Haltung heraus annahm.
   Um einen genaueren Einblick in unsere Überlegungen zu geben, habe
ich einige bezeichnende Gedanken und Überlegungen aus dem Ausstellungskatalog ausgewählt:
   „André Breton ging nach Mexiko wie in ein Traumland, auf der Suche nach
dem magischen Schnittpunkt von Kunst und Politik, ‚in dessen Verlängerung,
so hoffen wir, sich beide in ein und demselben revolutionären Bewußtsein
vereinigen, ohne daß es deshalb zu einer Vermischung ihrer im Wesen durchaus
verschiedenen Triebkräfte kommt‘ [Breton]. [...] Bretons Hoffnung auf eine dia-
lektische Einheit von Kunst und Revolution geistert durch die gesamte Moderne.
Daß es auch für uns heute noch eine bloße Hoffnung ist, zeigt, wie wenig

dauerhaft die von Breton und Vertretern anderer Richtungen gesuchten Lösungen
waren. Der anfängliche Elan hat sich nicht gehalten und wurde nicht zum
Gemeingut. Uns ist eine Reihe von Talismanen geblieben, die an bestimmten
Orten und zu bestimmten Zeiten zumeist gehäuft auftreten – die sowjetische
Kunst der ersten Jahre nach der Revolution, der Berliner Dadaismus, der französische Surrealismus, die mexikanische Renaissance –, auf die wir zur Ermutigung
und zum besseren Verständnis zurückgreifen können. [...] Warum Mexiko?
Eine Ausstellung der Arbeiten von Frida Kahlo und Tina Modotti wirft automatisch
die Frage nach der ‚Marginalität‘ auf, dem Status, der der mexikanischen Kunst
ebenso wie der Kunst von Frauen und (in Modottis Fall) der Photographie von
der etablierten Kunst, wie sie sich in Büchern und Museumsbeständen niederschlägt, zugewiesen wird. Die Zentren der Kunstgeschichte liegen in Europa
und den USA; Paris und New York sind die letzten Glieder einer Kette, die über
Rom und Florenz in die klassischen Kulturen der Antike zurückreicht. Brüche und
Abweichungen werden übergangen oder in Klammern gesetzt, das Heterogene
nur als ‚Einfluß‘ erwähnt. Auf diese Weise sind die Originalität, Breite und Fülle
der mexikanischen Kunst übersehen oder unterschätzt worden.“[4]

„Der zweite Bereich von Marginalität, den diese Ausstellung thematisiert,
ist der einer Kunst, die von Frauen gemacht wird. Dabei steht nicht mehr der
historische Zusammenhang, der Tina Modotti und Frida Kahlo beeinflußte,
im Mittelpunkt des Interesses, sondern die Diskussion über eine feministische
Ästhetik. An diesem Punkt wird die Gegenüberstellung der beiden Frauen
wichtig. Jede Ausstellung einer Künstlerin allein hätte ihre individuelle Bedeutung
hervorgehoben, ihren spezifischen Beitrag zu einer künstlerischen Technik
(Photographie bzw. Malerei) und den kulturellen Traditionen der Frau. Der Entschluß, das Werk von Tina Modotti und Frida Kahlo zusammen auszustellen,
beruht nicht allein auf der Tatsache, daß beide zu Unrecht vernachlässigt wurden
und ihr Leben und ihre Kunst von großem Interesse sind. Ihr Vergleich fördert
die Diskussion einer Reihe von Konzepten und Streitfragen, die für die Kunst von
Frauen und eine feministische Ästhetik relevant sind. [...] Andererseits [geht es
um] die Auseinandersetzung mit den Wertsetzungen, die durch die Spaltung in
reine und angewandte Kunst entstehen, sowie die Untersuchung des Prinzips,
das dieser scheinbar unüberbrückbaren Kluft zugrundeliegt. In unserem Zusammenhang wird dieser Aspekt ergänzt durch die Entdeckung der mexikanischen
Volkskunst während dieser Periode (der Hintergrund von Kahlos Werk) sowie

---

4   Laura Mulvey und Peter Wollen: „Frida Kahlo und Tina Modotti“, übersetzt von Karin
     Monte, in: *Frida Kahlo und Tina Modotti*, hg. von Mark Francis, Frankfurt am Main:
     Verlag Neue Kritik 1982, S. 7.

die Sehnsucht der Avantgarde, die Kunst in einen Dialog mit der modernen
Welt und ihrer Technologie zu bringen (ein entscheidender Faktor für Modotti,
die Photographie als politische Reportage zu verwenden)."[5]

In theoretischer Hinsicht befasste sich die Ausstellung *Frida Kahlo and Tina
Modotti* mit zentralen Fragen in Bezug auf Frauen und Kunst, die damals zum
ersten Mal gestellt wurden. Die vielleicht wichtigsten waren: erstens die Infrage-
stellung der traditionellen männlichen Dominanz in der Kunst, der high art
sowie des Konzepts des männlichen ‚Genies‘; und zweitens eine ‚archäologische‘
Suche nach den verlorenen Werken von Künstlerinnen, die Wiederentdeckung
ihrer vergessenen Geschichten. Dies ist ein Moment, den Sheila Rowbotham in
ihrem 1973 erschienenen Buch *Woman's Consciousness, Man's World* beschreibt.
Sie schreibt: „Die Unterdrückten ohne Hoffnung sind auf geheimnisvolle Weise
still. Wenn die Vorstellung von Veränderung jenseits der Grenzen des Möglichen
liegt, gibt es keine Worte, um die Unzufriedenheit zu artikulieren, sodass sie
manchmal als nicht existent angesehen wird. Dieser Irrglaube entsteht, weil wir
die Stille nur in dem Moment begreifen können, in dem sie sich Bahn bricht."[6]
Und in dieser Zeit beginnt das Aufbrechen der alten Stille. Ein anderer Buchtitel
von Rowbotham macht dies deutlich: *Hidden from History: 300 Years of
Women's Oppression and the Fight Against It* (ebenfalls 1973 erschienen).[7] Linda
Nochlin leitete die feministische Arbeit zur Wiederentdeckung verlorener
und vergessener Künstlerinnen mit ihrem Essay „Why Have There Been No Great
Women Artists?" ein, der erstmals 1971 in *ARTnews* veröffentlicht und im Laufe
der Jahrzehnte regelmäßig neu aufgelegt wurde.[8] Sie wies darauf hin, dass es
bei der Suche nach der Vergangenheit nicht nur um Entdeckung und Aufzählung
gehen könne, sondern um die Erforschung der historischen, sozialen und wirt-
schaftlichen Bedingungen, die Frauen von der elitären Welt männlicher Kreativität
ausgeschlossen hatten. Es war wichtig zu verstehen, dass, wenn es einigen
Künstlerinnen gelang, in diese Welt halbwegs einzudringen, sie dann schnell
wieder von ihr vergessen wurden. Nochlins einflussreicher Aufsatz führte 1976
zu der Ausstellung *Women Artists 1550–1950*, die durch die USA reiste und das
Thema buchstäblich auf den Radar brachte. Frida Kahlo war eine der 83 Künstlerinnen, die in dieser Ausstellung gezeigt wurden. 1979, drei Jahre vor unserer
Ausstellung, hatte Peter bereits gespürt, dass die Marginalisierung von Frauen

---

5 Ebd., S. 9.

6 Sheila Rowbotham: *Woman's Consciousness, Man's World*, London: Pelican 1973, S. 29.

7 Siehe Sheila Rowbotham: *Hidden from History: 300 Years of Women's Oppression
   and the Fight Against It*, London: Pluto Press 1973.

8 Siehe Linda Nochlin: "Why Have There Been No Great Women Artists?", in: *ARTnews*,
   Januar 1971, S. 22–39 und 67–71.

– nicht nur von Kahlo und Modotti – auch andere Formen von Einschränkungen widerspiegelt: „Die meisten Diskussionen über die Avantgarde sind sowohl eurozentrisch (oder nordamerika-zentriert) als auch männerzentriert. Zwei Künstlerinnen, die in Mexiko leben und arbeiten, können also eine andere Perspektive vermitteln."[9] Ich sollte auch erwähnen, dass der Geist hinter diesen Projekten vergleichbare Recherchen zu Filmen von Frauen inspiriert hat, die wiederum zu Festivals mit wiederentdeckten Werken geführt haben. Meine Beteiligung an der Frauenveranstaltung des Edinburgh Film Festivals im Jahr 1972 ist nur ein Beispiel dafür.[10]

Im Vereinigten Königreich wurde die Frage nach vergessenen Künstlerinnen von Rozsika Parker und Griselda Pollock in ihrem Buch *Old Mistresses: Women, Art and Ideology* (1981) sowie von Germaine Greer *The Obstacle Race: The Fortunes of Women Painters and Their Work* (1979) verfolgt. 1973 gründeten Ursula Owen und Carmen Callil den Verlag Virago Press, der sich schnell zu einem wichtigen Publikationsorgan für die feministische Bewegung entwickelte. Über ihre Motivation sagte Owen: „Das Schweigen. Das vielleicht wichtigste Thema unserer frühen Veröffentlichungen war die Abwesenheit der Stimmen und Erfahrungen von Frauen in der Kultur. Wir wollten Bücher über Leben veröffentlichen, die unsichtbar waren, und über Gefühle, die undenkbar gewesen waren."

All diese Initiativen bildeten den Hintergrund für unsere Überlegungen und Planungen zur Ausstellung.

*

Peter und ich schrieben den Katalogtext gemeinsam, wobei wir Verantwortung für verschiedene Abschnitte übernahmen, aber die Autor*innenschaft im Text nicht kennzeichneten. Wenn ich jetzt auf den Katalog zurückblicke, wird mir klar, dass der Kontrast zwischen den beiden Künstlerinnen zunehmend unsere gemeinsame Vorstellungskraft und unser Interesse weckte. Die Organisation der Ausstellung verlief einigermaßen reibungslos. Zu diesem Zeitpunkt, vor Frida Kahlos späteren Aufstieg zu Weltberühmtheit, waren die Sammler*innen bereit, ihre Kunstwerke zu verleihen. Es half auch, dass die Whitechapel Gallery eine kleine, aber angesehene Institution war. Im Fall von Tina Modotti stammten ihre

---

9 Peter Wollen: „Mexico / Women / Art", erstmals veröffentlicht in Emma Tennant (Hrsg.), *Saturday Night Reader,* London: 1979, nachgedruckt in Wollen: *Readings and Writings. Semiotic Counter Strategies*, London: Verso 1982, S. 105–122: 110.
10 Siehe das Dossier über den EFF 1972 in *Speaking Up. Remake. Frankfurter Frauenfilmtage 2018. Eine Publikation*, Hrsg. Heide Schlüpmann / Andrea Haller, Frankfurt 2018, S. 180–198.

Fotografien alle von der Fondazione Modotti in Udine, ihrer Heimatstadt. Die
Fondazione war unter der Schirmherrschaft von Vittorio Vidali gegründet worden,
einem Aktivisten der Kommunistischen Partei und Tinas letztem Liebhaber.

Es gab jedoch auch eine Beinahe-Katastrophe. Dolores Olmedo, eine sehr
reiche und einflussreiche Kunstkennerin in Mexiko-Stadt, war Sammlerin von
Werken von Diego Rivera und auch von Frida Kahlo. Sie hatte beide persönlich
gekannt. Für die feministische Ausrichtung der Ausstellung hatten jene Gemälde,
die ich als die ‚abjekten Kahlos‘ bezeichnete, eine besondere Bedeutung,
und die wichtigsten davon befanden sich in der Sammlung von Dolores Olmedo.
Es handelt sich dabei um Gemälde, die den weiblichen Körper auf eindringliche
und gewagte Weise als Ort des Leidens, entblößten Fleisches, von Geburts-
blutungen, Abtreibung und männlicher Gewalt darstellen. Während Kahlos Selbstporträts eine Art maskenhafte Äußerlichkeit aufweisen, machen die ‚abjekten
Bilder‘ das Verborgene und Unsagbare, also das Verdrängte, das sich hinter dieser
rätselhaften Schönheit verbirgt, schmerzhaft deutlich. Peter und Mark Francis
empfanden es als wichtig, Dolores Olmeda zu treffen und sich zu vergewissern,
dass diese Gemälde verfügbar sein würden. Während Peter sich in Mexiko auf-
hielt, um die Ausstellung vorzubereiten, besuchte er sie in ihrem Haus in Mexiko-
Stadt. Sie sagte: „Ich habe gerade ein sehr teures Werk von Diego Rivera bei
Sotheby‘s in New York gekauft. Um es zu bezahlen, musste ich die Kahlo-Gemälde
verpfänden.“ Diese Gemälde befanden sich bei den Pfandleihern in Mexiko,
und das Ticket lag bei Sotheby‘s. Ich kann mich leider nicht mehr daran erinnern,
wie das Problem gelöst wurde, aber es wurde gelöst – zu unserer großen
Erleichterung hatten wir die ‚abjekten Bilder‘ in unserer Ausstellung.

*

Kommen wir nun zum Film. Wir hatten eigentlich immer vor, ausgehend von der
Ausstellung einen Film zu machen. Zwischen dem Ende der Ausstellung und
dem Dreh des Films lag jedoch eine Zeitspanne, in der sich unsere Ideen deutlich
geklärt haben und der Dialog zwischen den beiden Künstlerinnen ausgeprägter
wurde, was letztlich die Form und Struktur des Films bestimmte. Um diesen Übergang zu verdeutlichen: Die Ausstellung bestand natürlich aus Kahlos Gemälden
und Modottis Fotografien an den Galeriewänden. Im begleitenden Katalogtext
haben wir unser Interesse am Leben der beiden Frauen und ihrer Politik, ihrer
Einstellung zum weiblichen Körper und den bedeutenden, aber sehr unterschiedlichen Fragen, die sie zur Kunst und Ästhetik von Frauen aufwerfen, erläutert.
Die Ideen und Bilder nahmen zwangsläufig unterschiedliche Räume ein. Im Film
war es hingegen möglich, diese Ideen zu einer anderen Art von Textur zu

verweben: Begriffe konnten den entsprechenden Werken gegenübergestellt und die verschiedenen Themen systematisch zu einem ‚dialogischen' Muster angeordnet werden.

Der Film wurde vom Arts Council of Great Britain finanziert. Traditionell finanzierte der ACGB Dokumentarfilme über Kunst und Künstler, die in öffentlichen, vor allem pädagogischen Einrichtungen wie großen Museen und Kunstgalerien gezeigt wurden. Zu diesem Zeitpunkt durfte die Tate Gallery, Großbritanniens führendes Museum für moderne Kunst, per Dekret keine reproduzierbaren Bilder in ihre Sammlung aufnehmen – keine Fotografien, keine Arbeiten von Filmemacher*innen.[11] In den 1970er Jahren begann der Arts Council, ausgehend von der bereits erwähnten experimentellen Arbeit der britischen Filmbewegung, diese Grenzen zu verwischen. Er begann, experimentelle Filmemacher*innen mit der Produktion von Dokumentarfilmen über Kunst und Künstler*innen zu beauftragen, die jedoch von den früheren, streng konventionellen Bildungsformaten abweichen sollten. Aus dieser doppelten Situation heraus verfolgte *Frida Kahlo and Tina Modotti* eine doppelte ästhetische Strategie. Zunächst hatten wir gehofft, dass Bedeutung einzig aus der Montage von Bildern entstehen würde und diese dem dokumentarischen Zweck des Auftrags angemessen wäre.

Letztendlich setzte sich jedoch der pädagogische Auftrag durch. Wir fügten einen Voice-over-Text hinzu, der größtenteils dem Ausstellungskatalog entnommen war, um die Bedeutung des Films und die Geschichten der Künstlerinnen für ein Publikum, das mit experimentellen Filmen nicht vertraut ist, klarer und leichter verständlich zu machen. Ich stehe dieser Entscheidung immer noch zwiespältig gegenüber. Andererseits haben wir es abgelehnt, die Kunstwerke mit Kamerabewegungen zu erkunden und die – vielleicht verlockende – Beziehung zwischen Film und Kunst zu nutzen, um Details zu entdecken und bei ihnen zu verweilen. Hinter dieser Entscheidung steht Peters und mein gemeinsames Streben nach Symmetrie und Struktur in all unseren Filmen. Für uns beide hatte die Symmetrie eine ästhetische, modernistische Anziehungskraft. In *Tina*

---

11 Über die Politik der Tate, keine reproduzierbaren Werke zu sammeln: „Im Vergleich zu ihren internationalen Pendants wie dem Centre Pompidou in Paris oder dem Museum of Modern Art in New York, die beide über bedeutende Fotosammlungen verfügen, hatte die Tate jahrelang gezögert, ob die Fotografie zu ihrem Aufgabenbereich gehören sollte. Erst mit der Eröffnung der Tate Modern im Jahr 2000 wurden schließlich eigene Fotoausstellungen in das Programm aufgenommen, die zunächst von externen Kuratoren ausgewählt und von Ausstellungen im Ausland übernommen wurden." Interview mit Simon Baker, der 2010 als erster Kurator für Fotografie der Tate ernannt wurde, *Financial Times*, 15. Mai 2015.

Modotti and Frida Kahlo dominiert die Struktur und zieht sich durch den gesamten Film. Jedes ordnende Thema kehrt zu einem gemeinsamen Ausgangspunkt zurück: dem Titelblatt, das Julian Rothenstein für jedes Kapitel entworfen hat. Die beiden Künstlerinnen werden in ihrem gemeinsamen Kontext, der Kunst und Politik des postrevolutionären Mexikos, einander gegenübergestellt, aber durch eine binäre Struktur von Gegensätzen kontrastiert.

Auf der Filmleinwand konnten die Bilder, Geschichten und Ideen, die im Galerieraum in der Luft schwebten, zu einer Reihe von visuellen Gegenüberstellungen verschmelzen und einen viel lebendigeren Dialog zwischen den beiden Künstlerinnen schaffen. Obwohl unsere früheren Filme alle auf der Grundlage von Montage aufgebaut waren (vor allem aufgrund des Stellenwerts von Mustern und Tableaus in ihrer Struktur), war die Gegenüberstellung sowohl in Form als auch Inhalt für *Frida Kahlo and Tina Modotti* entscheidend. Die Montage eröffnet einen Raum für eine ‚dritte Bedeutung‘, in der durch Kahlo und Modotti selbst das Leben der Frauen, ihre Kämpfe und die Besonderheit ihrer Kunst im Allgemeinen nachhallen.

Die Gemälde von Kahlo und die Fotografien von Modotti sind thematisch in drei Kapitel gegliedert. Dazwischen gibt es zwei Abschnitte, die sich mit dem Leben und dem Bild der Künstlerinnen beschäftigen: ‚Wurzeln / Bewegung‘, ‚Biografie‘, ‚Innen / Außen‘, ‚Der Körper‘, ‚Verletzung / Schönheit‘. In allen Kapiteln wird ein Kontrast zwischen Kahlos beharrlicher Rückbesinnung auf die eigene Malerei und Modottis Auseinandersetzung mit dem öffentlichen Raum hergestellt. Im Nachhinein erscheint diese binäre Struktur ziemlich verkürzt.[12] Ich erinnere mich jedoch daran, dass wir bei der Ausarbeitung des Films sehr viel über Montage und Eisenstein nachgedacht haben, sowohl in Bezug auf seine Filmtheorie als auch auf seine Beziehung zu Mexiko, obwohl beides im Film selbst nicht vorkommt. In den Abschnitten ‚Biografie‘ und ‚Der Körper‘ geht es um das Leben von Kahlo und Modotti. Da es für den Film so wichtig war, ihr künstlerisches Schaffen in den Kontext ihrer Erfahrungen zu stellen, die in der Ausstellung in den Katalogtext verbannt wurden, werde ich in diesem abschließenden Teil meines Vortrags einer jeweils kurzen biografischen Darstellung der beiden

---

12 Es wäre falsch, Frida Kahlo trotz ihrer Verletzungen, die sie in ihrer Bewegungsfreiheit einschränkten, und trotz ihrer starken Bindung an ihre Heimat und ihr Land als durchgehend abgeschottet oder zurückgezogen zu betrachten. In mancher Hinsicht könnte man die ‚Verwurzelung‘ Frida Kahlos leicht übertreiben. Tatsächlich reiste sie viel durch die Vereinigten Staaten, zunächst mit Rivera, dann auf eigene Faust, als sie als eigenständige Malerin anerkannt wurde, und auch aus medizinischen Gründen. Sie reiste nach Europa, nachdem André Breton voller Begeisterung für ihr Werk nach Paris zurückgekehrt war.

widmen. Um auf die relative Abgeschiedenheit von Kahlos Leben zu verweisen,
schweift die Kamera durch das Blaue Haus, in dem sie geboren wurde und bis
zu ihrem Tod lebte; die Kommentarstimme erwähnt den Unfall in ihrer Kindheit,
der sie für den Rest ihres Lebens mit Schmerzen kämpfen ließ und so zwangsläufig zu einem ausgeprägten Bewusstsein für ihren Körper führte. Wir verknüpf-
ten diesen Umstand mit einigen der wiederkehrenden Themen ihrer Kunst,
in denen sie sich selbst zum Hauptgegenstand macht. Ihre Gemälde sind auch
eine materielle Manifestation ihrer inneren Erfahrungen, Träume und Fantasien
und scheinen als ‚Dekoration‘ ihres Lebens und ihrer Beziehungen zu fungieren,
ähnlich wie sie sich und ihr Haus mit den Farben und Objekten der mexikanischen Volkskunst schmückte.

Der Abschnitt zu Tina Modotti zeigt eine Reihe von Karten und zeichnet
die Reisen nach, die ihr Leben geprägt haben: In Italien geboren, emigrierte sie
mit ihrer Familie in die Vereinigten Staaten, zog von San Francisco nach Los
Angeles und dann von Kalifornien nach Mexiko. Aus politischen Gründen aus
Mexiko ausgewiesen, gelangte sie über Rotterdam nach Europa, suchte dann
politisches Asyl in Berlin, bis sie aufgrund der sich verschlechternden politischen
Lage nach Moskau flüchtete. Als Agentin der Komintern wurde sie nach Paris
geschickt, dann nach Spanien und nach der Niederlage der Republik gegen
Franco und die faschistischen Kräfte im Bürgerkrieg wieder nach Frankreich.
Schließlich kehrte sie nach Mexiko zurück, wo sie 1942 im Alter von nur fünfund-
vierzig Jahren starb.

Modotti hat die Räumlichkeiten, in denen sie lebte, nicht dekoriert. Manuel
Alvarez Bravo erinnert sich: „Die Wände ihres Ateliers waren weiß und sauber.
Später begann sie, einige Phrasen von Lenin und Marx darauf zu schreiben."[13]
Die etwa zehn Jahre, die sie in Mexiko verbrachte (erster Besuch 1922, ein zweiter
mehr oder weniger fester Aufenthalt von 1923 bis 1930, das endgültige Exil von
April 1939 bis zu ihrem Tod), waren der längste Zeitraum, den sie während ihres
Erwachsenenlebens in einem einzigen Land verbrachte. Es ist auch die Zeit,
in der fast ihre gesamte fotografische Arbeit entstand.

Nach ihrer Ausweisung aus Mexiko legte das Schiff, mit dem Tina Modotti
deportiert wurde, in New Orleans an, wo sie acht Tage lang in der dortigen
Einwanderungsstation festgehalten wurde. Sie schrieb an Weston:

„Die Zeitungen sind mir mit wölfischer Gier gefolgt und zeitweise vorausge-
gangen – hier in den USA wird alles unter dem Gesichtspunkt der ‚Schönheit‘
gesehen – eine Tageszeitung hier berichtete über meine Reise und bezeichnete
mich als ‚eine Frau von auffallender Schönheit‘ – andere Reporter, denen ich

---

13 Manuel Alvarez Bravo, zitiert in Constantine, *Tina Modotti: A Fragile Life*, 1975.

ein Interview verweigerte, versuchten mich zu überzeugen, indem sie sagten,
sie würden nur davon sprechen, ‚wie hübsch ich sei' – worauf ich antwortete,
dass ich bei bestem Willen nicht erkennen könne, was ‚Hübschheit' mit der
revolutionären Bewegung oder mit der Vertreibung von Kommunisten zu tun
habe – offensichtlich werden Frauen hier an einem Filmstandard gemessen."[14]

Die Entscheidungen, die Frida Kahlo und Tina Modotti bewusst oder unbe-
wusst trafen, waren eindeutig mit ihren eigenen Existenzbedingungen,
ihrer Klasse, ihrem Geschlecht, ihrer Geschichte und sogar mit dem Zufall ver-
knüpft – ein Zeichen für die kontingenten Aspekte der Arbeit von Künstlerinnen,
die so leicht durch Vorstellungen von Genialität verschleiert werden. Um es zum
Abschluss noch einmal zu wiederholen: Diese Verbindung zwischen Geschichte
und Kontingenz, die Art und Weise, wie das Werk der beiden Künstlerinnen
sowohl von dem ihnen übergeordneten Kontext als auch von den Ereignissen
ihres Lebens beeinflusst wurde, war für Peter und mich eine wichtige Über-
legung, als wir am Ausstellungskatalog arbeiteten. Es galt schon seit einer Weile
als unzeitgemäß, über Kunst und Künstler*innen aus einer biografischen Perspektive zu schreiben. Aber im Falle von Frauen, ihren Leistungen und ihrer
öffentlichen Präsenz schien es politisch und ästhetisch unmöglich, ihre persön-
lichen und individuellen Erfahrungen zu ignorieren. Im Film konnten wir diese
komplizierten Wechselwirkungen stärker in den Vordergrund rücken: Die Lebens-
geschichten von Frida Kahlo und Tina Modotti bilden eine wesentliche Ebene
in der Gesamtstruktur des Films und beeinflussen die Gegensätze, die die anderen
Abschnitte miteinander verbinden und verflechten. Indem wir diese beiden
Künstlerinnen an den Wänden der Whitechapel Gallery, im Katalogtext und im
Film zusammenbrachten, hofften Peter und ich, ihre Kunst, ihre Leistungen
und den Kontext der mexikanischen Avantgarde zu feiern. Aber wir hofften auch,
ein feministisches Prinzip zu artikulieren und sichtbar zu machen: Was Kahlo
und Modotti tun wollten und was für sie möglich war, ihre Wünsche und Grenzen,
wurden durch die Tatsache definiert, dass sie Frauen waren.

*Eine Version dieses Textes wurde von Laura Mulvey am 8. November 2022 im
Cabaret Voltaire in Zürich präsentiert.*

---

14 Brief von Tina Modotti an Edward Weston, zitiert in Constantine, *Tina Modotti: A Fragile
    Life*, S. 175.

FRIDA KAHLO AND TINA MODOTTI

Peter Wollen
Fridamania

Die erste Retrospektive von Frida Kahlos Werk außerhalb Mexikos eröffnete
im Mai 1982 in der Whitechapel Gallery in London. Sie wurde von Laura
Mulvey und mir organisiert und kuratiert. Es handelte sich um eine
Gemeinschaftsausstellung mit Arbeiten von Kahlo und Tina Modotti,
der italienisch-amerikanisch-mexikanischen Fotografin, die später selbst
zum Gegenstand einer kleinen „Tinamania" wurde. Damals lehnten
Mulvey und ich Ausstellungen ab, die sich auf das Schaffen eines einzigen
Künstlers oder einer einzigen Künstlerin beschränkten und hielten die
Gegenüberstellung zweier verwandter Werkgruppen für aufschlussreicher
als eine in sich abgeschlossene Einzelausstellung. Außerdem wollten
wir Fotografie und Malerei gleichberechtigt ausstellen. Nach der Eröffnung
in Whitechapel reiste die Ausstellung nach Deutschland und Stockholm,
bevor sie weiter in die Grey Art Gallery in New York und schließlich
in das Nationale Kunstmuseum in Mexiko-Stadt zog. Die nordamerikani-
schen Ausstellungsorte kamen erst nach der Eröffnung und aufgrund
der Resonanz, die die Ausstellung in Europa fand, hinzu. Dies hatte zur
Folge, dass Kahlos Werk in den USA – genauer: in der künstlerischen
und intellektuellen Hauptstadt New York – im Jahr 1983 bekannt wurde,
was ungefähr mit dem Erscheinen ihrer Biografie von Hayden Herreras
zusammenfällt. Ich glaube, dass das Zusammenwirken dieser beiden
Ereignisse – die Ausstellung und das Buch – in den USA ein Interesse
weckte, das sich später mit der Begeisterung in Europa und Mexiko
verband und zur „Fridamania" führte: der Erhöhung von Kahlo zum
Kultobjekt.
Seitdem folgte eine Reihe weiterer Ausstellungen, Kataloge, Bücher
– und später auch Postkarten, Kalender, Wandplakate, Stellwände,
Tagebücher und Spielfilme, zunächst von Paul Leduc und jetzt von Julie
Taymor. Innerhalb eines Jahrzehnts wurde Frida Kahlo zu einer der
wahrscheinlich bekanntesten Künstlerinnen der Welt. Wie konnte das
geschehen? Und warum? Wie wir sehen werden, führen diese Fragen
zu weiteren Aspekten, die für die Geschichte des Geschmacks und der
Kunstrezeption, sowie allgemein für die Entstehung kultureller Ikonen
von Bedeutung sind.

In Coyoacán

Zunächst die Frage, warum wir die Ausstellung überhaupt organisieren
wollten: Das mag an Selbstdarstellung grenzen, ist aber vielleicht passend,
wenn man über eine Künstlerin wie Kahlo schreibt. Wir waren keine
Kunsthistoriker*innen und hatten noch nie eine Kunstausstellung organisiert. Wir waren Filmtheoretiker*innen und Avantgarde-Filme-
macher*innen. In den Weihnachtsferien 1978/79 fuhren wir gemeinsam
nach Mexiko und wohnten bei einem Freund, der am Colegio de México
politische Geschichte Japans lehrte. Zuvor hatte ich Kahlos Gemälde
„Porträt von Frida und Diego" in der historischen Ausstellung „Women
Artists: 1550–1950" gesehen, die 1976 von Ann Sutherland Harris und
Linda Nochlin organisiert wurde. Bei der Planung meiner Reise spielte
Kahlo jedoch kaum eine Rolle. In den Büchern, die ich mir ansah,
gab es nur spärliche Informationen – Riveras Ehefrau; hat ein paar Bilder
gemalt. Ihre Rolle wurde mir erst nach meiner Ankunft in Mexiko-Stadt
bewusst. Auf den von Rivera gemalten Wandgemälden im Innenhof
des Bildungsministeriums in Mexiko-Stadt wird sie – zusammen mit Tina
Modotti – als Revolutionärin dargestellt, die Waffen an die Arbeiter
und Bauern verteilt. Um Trotzkis Haus zu besichtigen, fuhren wir in den
Vorort Coyoacán. Das Blaue Haus, das Kahlo gehörte, befand sich in
der Nähe, und so beschlossen wir, auch dieses zu besuchen. Wie sich heraus-
stellte, sollte uns das Blaue Haus nachhaltiger beeindrucken.

Tatsächlich gab es dort nur einen einzigen Raum mit Werken von Kahlo
– keineswegs ihren besten. Die Wirkung ging vom Haus selbst aus.
Wenn ich zurückdenke, reihe ich es gedanklich in eine Serie ein, zu der
auch die Gaudí-Häuser in Barcelona (insbesondere die Casa Batlló
und das Dach der Pedrera) und die Watts Towers in Los Angeles gehören.
Gaudí hatte ich auf eine gewisse Art bereits über das Drehbuch zu
Antonionis Film *The Passenger* ‚ausgestellt', das ich einige Jahre zuvor
gemeinsam mit Mark Peploe verfasst hatte. Einige Szenen in diesem Film
spielen in Gaudí-Gebäuden. Generell interessierte ich mich für eine
bestimmte, äußerst persönliche oder „Außenseiter"-Architektur. Das tue
ich immer noch. Dieses Interesse geht auf den Surrealismus zurück.
So überrascht es nicht, dass es André Breton war, der Kahlo als Malerin
„entdeckte‟, den Aufsatz für den Katalog ihrer ersten New Yorker Ausstellung (1939, in der Julien Levy Gallery) schrieb und im selben Jahr eine
Ausstellung ihrer Arbeiten in Paris organisierte. Breton sorgte persönlich dafür, dass ihr Werk im Ausland gesehen wurde und als Surrealistin

(oder Parasurrealistin) wurde sie ursprünglich außerhalb – und bis zu
einem gewissen Grad auch innerhalb – Mexikos wahrgenommen.

Der „Außenseiter"-Aspekt des Blauen Hauses hatte neben seiner Bezie-
hung zum Surrealismus noch eine weitere wichtige Eigenschaft. Das Blaue
Haus stand in krassem Gegensatz zu den weißen Wänden, den leeren
Räumen und dem techno-hygienischen Erscheinungsbild eines typischen
Museums für moderne Kunst. Der Raum war ungeordnet, heimisch, farben-
froh und voller eigenartiger Objekte. Für mich stellte Kahlo in vielerlei
Hinsicht die orthodoxen Doktrinen der Moderne in Frage. Zum einen war sie
eine Künstlerin und es galt als bekannt, dass Frauen in der Geschichte des
Modernismus eine untergeordnete Rolle spielten. Zweitens war sie in ge-
wissem Sinne eine ‚Außenseiterin', eine unausgebildete, nicht professionelle
Künstlerin, die aus eigenem Antrieb malte, ohne ausstellen zu wollen; und
auch das drängte sie, im Verhältnis zum Mainstream der Kunstwelt, in eine
marginale Position. Drittens stammte sie aus Mexiko, einem Land außerhalb des kulturell dominierenden europäisch-amerikanischen Raums.
Viertens hatte sie Verbindungen zum Surrealismus, der in der Geschichte der
Moderne zwar anerkannt war, in der rationalistischen Bauhaus-Tradition
der Kunstgeschichte wie auch in der Darstellung der „Kunst um der
Kunst willen" von Greenberg immer noch etwas verdächtig erschien.
Ich interessierte mich auch für die Tragweite ihres politischen Engagements
– für Trotzki, aber auch für den orthodoxen Kommunismus.

Nach dem Besuch des Blauen Hauses versuchte ich gezielter, Arbeiten
von Kahlo zu sehen. Entscheidend war wahrscheinlich, dass ich kurz
darauf die im Museum für Moderne Kunst im Chapultepec Park ausge-
stellten Bilder sah. Vor allem die beiden Fridas, ihr sicherlich ehrgeizigstes
mir zugängliches Werk. Nach meiner Rückkehr nach London schlugen
wir der Whitechapel Gallery eine Ausstellung vor – ein Projekt, das vom
Direktor und von Mark Francis, dem zuständigen Kurator des Hauses,
akzeptiert wurde. Ich reiste mehrmals nach Mexiko, zunächst allein
und dann mit Mark Francis, um alle Werke ausfindig zu machen und die
Leihgaben zu sichern. In dieser Zeit lernte ich durch gemeinsame
Freund*innen Hayden Herrera kennen; wir konnten uns austauschen,
auch wenn ich mehr von ihr lernte als sie von mir. Obwohl ihr Buch
erst nach der Ausstellung erschien, war ihre Arbeit zu diesem Punkt bereits
viel weiter fortgeschritten als meine. In dieser Zeit schrieb ich auch ein
Stück, eine Mischung aus Fiktion und Essay, mit dem Titel „Mexico /
Women / Art", das 1979 in London im Saturday Night Reader, einem von
Emma Tennant herausgegebenen Sammelband, veröffentlicht wurde.

Vor kurzem habe ich diesen Beitrag nach vielen Jahren wieder gelesen
und war über meine Argumentationsweise erstaunt. Im ersten Absatz
werden Rivera und der Muralismus, Breton und der Surrealismus, Trotzki
und der revolutionäre Kommunismus genannt. Im Mittelpunkt steht
jedoch „ihr unerbittlicher Kampf gegen Verletzungen und Krankheiten".
Wie wir sehen werden, war dies ein entscheidendes Element bei der
Konstruktion der Kahlo-Legende. Weiter betone ich die „nicht-westlichen"
(oder „Dritte-Welt-") Aspekte von Kahlos Kunst und vergleich Mexiko
mit dem Iran, einem Land, in dem ich einige Zeit gelebt hatte. Ich war
mit der Geschichte des Modernismus und der Frage beschäftigt, was die
Idee einer „Avantgarde" ausmachen könnte – Themen, die für mich
auch aus meiner Arbeit als Filmemacher hervorgegangen sind. Zugleich war
ich fasziniert von Kahlos Verwendung von populärer Kunst und Bild-
sprache, insbesondere von den Ex-Voto-Gemälden, die sie sammelte und
die sich direkt auf ihre eigene Krankengeschichte beziehen lassen.
Ich interessierte mich dafür, wie die Avantgarde der Sechzigerjahre – zum
Beispiel die Fluxus-Bewegung – Themen der Zwanzigerjahre aufgriff –
Frauenkunst, politische Kunst, Fotografie, populäre Darstellungen,
Umwelt, Performance – und wie diese auch für Kahlo relevant waren.
Ein ganzer Abschnitt befasst sich mit Kahlos Verwendung der Tehuana-
Tracht und stellt eine Verbindung zum Feminismus, zur tragischen
Dimension des Körpers, zur „Kreolisierung" indigener Kulturen und zur
psychoanalytischen Theorie der Maskerade her.

Kultbildung

In gewisser Weise habe ich versucht, durch die Beschäftigung mit Kahlo
eine Theorie dessen zu entwickeln, was zu diesem Zeitpunkt noch nicht
Postmoderne genannt wurde; und zwar durch den Rekurs auf eine andere,
unterdrückte Seite der Moderne und unter Beibehaltung des sehr un-
postmodernen Konzepts der Avantgarde. Ich sah in Kahlo eine Vorläuferin
einer anderen Avantgarde als vorausgreifende kunstgeschichtliche
Mutation. Die Dinge, die mich an ihrem Werk interessierten, waren in vieler
Hinsicht dieselben, die auch zur Entstehung des Kahlo-Kults führten.
Als ich das Werk zum ersten Mal sah, hatte es für mich persönlich eine
unmittelbare Relevanz und eine starke Wirkung; in gewissem Sinne hätte
es mich also nicht überraschen dürfen, als sich die Arbeiten weiterver-
breiteten und eine ebenso starke Kraft auf andere ausstrahlten. Vielleicht

gilt dies umso mehr, da ich weder ein Kunsthistoriker noch ein Museums-
experte war. Auch ich war ein Laienbetrachter. Doch die Entstehung
eines Kults erfordert mehr als individuelle Bedeutung oder Wirkung,
so stark diese auch sein mag – und ich glaube, dass die Fridamania eine
Art Kult ist, der in seiner Tragweite und Intensität stellenweise wie
der klassische Kult der Jungfrau von Guadalupe (oder der Mater Dolorosa)
erscheint. Auch Kahlo hat ihre Anhänger*innen, ihre Verehrer*innen,
ihre Pilger*innen und sogar ihre Altare. Es müssen bestimmte Merkmale
in einem Werk vorhanden sein, die die Entstehung eines Kults begünstigen,
aber es muss noch etwas hinzukommen – eine Beziehung zwischen Werk
und Leben, ein bestimmter historischer Kontext. Es folgen einige Hypo-
thesen über die Entstehungsbedingungen eines Kults.

Erstens erstarkte der Feminismus und damit verbunden das Interesse
an der Kunst von Frauen. Einige Jahre vor der Ausstellung wurden
Kahlos Arbeiten in der Grey Gallery an der US-amerikanischen Westküste
(teilweise) in einem Chicana-Kontext gezeigt. Aber erst als weibliche
Malerin zog sie die öffentliche Aufmerksamkeit auf sich. In vielerlei Hinsicht war sie eine ideale Kandidatin für den Kultstatus. Sie lebte nicht
mehr, weshalb sie in einer Weise monumental war, die noch lebenden
Künstler*innen versperrt ist, ohne jedoch zu weit in der Vergangenheit zu
liegen. Sie starb 1954, noch in ihren frühen Vierzigern. Außerdem war sie
Mexikanerin – dies erlaubte es ihr, sowohl als Künstlerin *of colour* aus
„der dritten Welt" wahrgenommen zu werden, als auch als Künstlerin, die
sich das „Anderssein" Mexikos aneignete, um das vorgängige „Anderssein" als Frau zu verdoppeln. Sie stand im Schatten eines berühmteren
Ehemannes – wie Sophie Taeuber, Sonia Delaunay, Varvara Stepanova,
Gabriele Münter, Barbara Hepworth, Georgia O'Keeffe, Lee Krasner und
viele andere. In dieser Hinsicht war ihre Position typisch, in anderen
Punkten aber auch untypisch. Sie war eine, im wahrsten Sinne des Wortes,
verletzte Frau – durch ihre Beziehung zu Rivera auch psychisch.
Der Mythos der leidenden Künstlerin, der schon immer stark war, erfuhr
im Kontext des Feminismus eine Steigerung.

Zweitens fiel die Wiederentdeckung von Kahlo mit einer Wiederkehr der
figurativen Malerei in den 1970er Jahren zusammen: Kiefer, Immendorf,
Chia, Clemente, Salle, Fischl. Dies stand im Zusammenhang mit dem
Niedergang der Hochmoderne, der Ablehnung des Konzeptualismus und
dem Aufkommen des Postmodernismus. Diese Malerei war jedoch fast
ausschließlich eine Angelegenheit von Männern. Künstlerinnen bewegten
sich auf anderem Terrain – im Medium Fotografie, das von Kruger,

Sherman und anderen verwendet wurde. Kahlo schlug eine alternative
Bildtradition für Frauen vor, die durch ihre Wahl des Selbstporträts
als wichtigste Ausdrucksform zusätzlich an Kraft gewann. Ihre Kunst war
intim, privat und persönlich; es ging um ihre Identität als Frau und
Mexikanerin; es ging um den Körper – ganz konkret um den weiblichen
und noch spezifischer um ihren eigenen Körper; es ging um Kinder,
oder ihr Fehlen. Kleidung und ihre Bedeutung und das widersprüchliche
Verhältnis von Stärke und Schwäche. Sie stand in krassem Gegensatz
zur überheblichen Askese eines wesentlichen Teils der Spätmoderne,
zu ihrer prophetischen Leere, ihrem angestrengten Streben, hohe Kunst
zu sein und zu ihrer ultrafeinen Malstruktur. Obwohl Kahlos Gemälde
im Gegensatz zu vielen von Männern gemalten Bildern kleinformatig sind,
sind sie sowohl erschütternd als auch gewaltvoll in ihrer Erscheinung
und stechen sofort ins Auge. Teilweise setzten sie sich aufgrund ihrer bloßen
Qualität durch. Sie ließen sich auch gut reproduzieren, und das ist eher
ein Kompliment als ein Kritikpunkt.

Über den Kult der „leidenden Künstlerin" – ein Phänomen, das früheren
Kulten wie denen von Van Gogh oder Modigliani und sogar Judy Garland
oder Marilyn Monroe zugrunde liegt – muss mehr gesagt werden. Die
„leidende Künstlerin" war emotional besonders aufgeladen – persönliches
Leid und geschlechtliche Diskriminierung überlagern sich in einer Weise,
die eine starke psychische Identifikation mit der Kultfigur ermöglicht.
Selbstverständlich ist Kahlos Kunst viel komplexer als diese Beschrei-
bung vermuten lässt, aber Kulte beruhen nicht unbedingt auf Vielschichtig-
keit. Der Kult um Kahlo ähnelt in vielen Punkten dem um Sylvia Plath.
Auch sie wurde verletzt und ins Krankenhaus eingeliefert – wenn auch
eher aus psychischen als physischen Gründen – und lebte in einer zutiefst
ambivalenten und schmerzhaften Beziehung mit einem berühmteren
Ehemann. (Natürlich ändert sich der Bekanntheitsgrad im Laufe der Zeit.
Kahlo mag heute berühmter sein als Rivera, Modotti berühmter als
Weston. Ich glaube, dass in beiden Fällen ihre Werke heute mehr wert sind
als die ihrer Männer.) Die Energie, die das Interesse an Plath antreibt,
gründet offensichtlich in einem Zusammenspiel von Viktimisierung,
Schuldzuweisung, Unterwürfigkeit und Faszination für Gewalt, die sowohl
nach innen als auch nach außen gerichtet ist. Vergleichbares könnte man
auch über Kahlo sagen.

In beiden Fällen wird der Kult durch eine Vielzahl unterschiedlicher
Materialien aufrechterhalten: durch die Veröffentlichung von Werken,
Biografien, Briefsammlungen, privaten Tagebüchern, Kritiken, Fotobüchern,

Filmen und Fernsehsendungen sowie durch die entsprechenden Arbeiten
ihrer Ehemänner oder anderer nahestehender Personen. Dieser Quellen-
reichtum ermöglicht eine viel stärkere Identifikation, als es durch das
Werk allein möglich wäre. Die Bewunder*innen haben das Gefühl, das
Objekt ihrer Verehrung in einer detaillierten und intimen Weise zu
kennen, die ihnen privilegierte Einblicke in das Gefühlsleben des Idols
gewährt. Dabei handelt es sich nicht um eine bloße Anhäufung von
Nebensächlichkeiten: Je mehr Material über das Privatleben der Künstler*innen zugänglich gemacht wird, desto überzeugender wird das
Gefühl, dass man nachvollziehen kann, wie sich Kahlo oder Plath fühlten;
so, dass man sich mit ihren tiefsten und intimsten Gefühlen identifizieren
kann. Auch in diesem Sinne ist das Blaue Haus ein Ort mit einer großen
emotionalen Wirkung und darin vergleichbar mit Charleston oder dem
ebenfalls öffentlich zugänglichen Haus von Virginia Woolf, das zur
Stärkung des Bloomsbury-Kults beigetragen hat. Ein Kult beruht auf
dieser Art von Identifikation. Er kann sich selbst erhalten, da das Wachs-
tum des Kults sein eigenes Publikum für weitere Veröffentlichungen
erzeugt, die mit mehr Informationen, Bildern und Erläuterungen versorgt
werden müssen.

Verhüllung und Sichtbarmachung

Natürlich bleibt das persönliche Material, aus dem Kahlo beim Malen
schöpfte, wichtig und bedeutsam und keineswegs irrelevant für ihre
Kunst. Die Problematik besteht nur darin, dass gleichzeitig ein Streben
nach Vereinfachung auszumachen ist. In Wirklichkeit ist die Kunst von
Kahlo wie auch die von Plath ungewöhnlich komplex und widersprüchlich.
Das zeigt sich zum Beispiel an der Rolle, die Kahlos Kleidung in ihren
Selbstporträts und, wie wir aus Biografien und Fotografien wissen, in ihrer
Selbstdarstellung im Alltag spielt. Die Wahl der mexikanischen Tracht
und insbesondere der langen Röcke, reflektiert das Bedürfnis (oder den
Wunsch), ihre Wunden zu verbergen, die sie sich bei einem Verkehrsunfall
im Alter von achtzehn Jahren zugezogen hat. Eine Straßenbahn krachte
in den Bus, in dem sie unterwegs war. Kahlo wurde von einem zerbrochenen
Stück Stahlgeländer des vorderen Wagens der Tram getroffen. Ihre
Wirbelsäule war an drei Stellen gebrochen, zwei Rippen waren gebrochen,
ihr Becken war an drei Stellen gebrochen, ihr Schlüsselbein war gebrochen, ihr rechtes Bein hatte elf Brüche, ihr rechter Fuß war zerquetscht

und die linke Schulter ausgekugelt. Ihre Kleidung diente offensichtlich dazu, das Ausmaß ihrer Verletzungen zu verbergen. Die besondere Wahl der Bekleidung führte jedoch auch dazu, den oder die Betrachter*in an die Verletzungen zu erinnern, indem die Aufmerksamkeit durch eine Art „negative Darstellung" auf die wohlüberlegte Kleidungsauswahl gelenkt wurde. Kahlo verwendete ihre Kleider als äußerst vielschichtige Zeichen, die im Laufe der Zeit immer aufwendiger wurden.

Zunächst zeigte die Kleidung einfach ihr Mexikanischsein. Nach der mexikanischen Revolution in den 1920er Jahren war dies eine unproblematische Entscheidung. Kahlo legte jedoch ihr ganzes Leben lang Wert auf diesen Aspekt und wurde mit der Wahl der Tehuana-Tracht noch ein Stück extremer. Es hat den Anschein, dass sie ursprünglich Rivera gefallen wollte, der häufig den Isthmus von Tehuantepec besuchte und die Frauen dort malte. Kurz nach der Stabilisierung der revolutionären Lage kehrte Rivera aus Paris nach Mexiko zurück und wurde von seinem Gönner José Vasconcelos, dem damaligen Bildungsminister, für einen Besuch nach Tehuantepec geschickt. Vasconcelos wollte Rivera ent-europäisieren und ihm sein mexikanisches Bewusstsein zurückgeben. Er wählte Tehuantapec als repräsentativen Ort für eine unberührte und reiche indigene Kultur. Die Gegend war vor allem für die dort lebenden Frauen bekannt – sowohl für ihren Status als „starke Frauen" als auch für ihre auffälligen Trachten. (Sie waren auch für ihre ungenierte Nacktheit berühmt. Nackte Tehuanas, die im Fluss stehen, waren ein häufiges Motiv für folkloristische Fotografien.)

Rivera lernte Vasconcelos' Lektion und malte nach seiner Rückkehr auf den Wandbildern im Bildungsministerium Bilder von Tehuana-Frauen in voller Tracht. Er behielt sein künstlerisches Interesse an den Frauen des Isthmus bei und begrüßte es anscheinend, als Kahlo ihren Stil übernahm. Auf jeden Fall machte sie ihn sich zu eigen. Sie verband die Ikonographie der starken Frau, der Matriarchin, mit der des authentischen Mexikanischseins (zumindest der Legende nach) und machte aus der Not eine Tugend, indem sie aus der schützenden Verhüllung eine kämpferische und extravagante Zurschaustellung machte.

Rivera selbst war als Mythomane, als notorischer Lügner und Erfinder verblüffender Erzählungen, bekannt. Wie Kahlo bemerkte, war er eher ein Fabulierer im großen Stil als ein belangloser Betrüger. Er suchte beflissen die Öffentlichkeit und stellte bewusst ein imposanteres Bild von sich selbst zur Schau, als seinem Leben entsprach.

In diesem Sinne lernte Kahlo von Rivera, wie man eine wirksame öffentliche Legende von sich selbst erschafft. Die Tatsache, dass sie darauf

bedacht war, ihre eigene mythische Identität zu gestalten, deren zentrales
Element der Komplex Behinderung / Tehuana war, begünstigte noch
viele Jahre nach ihrem Tod die Entstehung eines Kults. Paradoxerweise
entfaltete ihre hochgradig zeichenhafte Selbstdarstellung ihre vollständige
Wirkung erst auf einer Art Metaebene – vor einem anderen Publikum
in einem anderen Kontext, der von dem von ihr vorgesehenen weit ent-
fernt war. Es ist wichtig zu betonen, dass Kahlos Selbstporträts von
einem sehr frühen Stadium an von Selbst-Fabulation durchdrungen sind.
Das Selbst, das sie porträtiert, ist ein konstruiertes und sorgfältig ent-
worfenes Selbst, das sich schließlich in den Bildern von Frida-als-Tehuana
herauskristallisiert, die sich das aneignet und für ihre eigenen Zwecke
gestaltet, was für sie, wie für Diego, und auch für uns, ein exotisches
Bild war.

Anfang der 1990er Jahre sah ich in Mexiko-Stadt eine Ausstellung
mit Bildern von Tehuana-Frauen von mexikanischen Malern vom frühen
neunzehnten Jahrhundert bis in die Gegenwart. Die Bildsprache, die
Kahlo verwendete, steht in der langen Bildtradition der Darstellung der
Tehuana und der Verehrung eines tropischen und weiblichen Mexiko.
Diese Bildsprache wandelte sich mit den Stilrichtungen der Kunst, aber
auch mit der veränderten Einstellung gegenüber dem Isthmus und dem
Süden. Verschiedene Künstler verwendeten das Motiv der Tehuana auf sehr
unterschiedliche Weise. Saturnino Herrán erinnert an die andalusische
Roma; Adolfo Best Maugard verbindet die Tehuana mit der indigenen
Houri; Roberto Montenegros Porträt von Rosa Rolando mit ihrem kunst-
vollen, das Gesicht umhüllenden Tehuana-Kopfschmuck ist ernst und
lässt sie wie die Vorsteherin eines Klosters aussehen. Rivera bevorzugt
Darstellungen von Männern und Frauen, die gemeinsam den *Sandunga*
tanzen und betont ihre hochmütige Zurückhaltung und Selbstbeherr-
schung. Tina Modotti zeigt (in ihren Fotografien) Frauen bei der Arbeit
oder mit Säuglingen und Kleinkindern; Miguel Covarrubias stilisiert
und akzentuiert die Indigenität, und so weiter. In jüngerer Zeit schlagen
die Fotografien von Graciela Iturbide und die Malerei von Julio Galán
einen exzentrischeren, grelleren und sogar grotesken Ton an.

Kahlo verwendet die Tehuana-Tracht ausdrücklich als eine Form
der Maskerade, die unterschiedliche und widersprüchliche Assoziationen
hervorruft: die Kostümierung als Zeichen für und gegen Weiblichkeit,
für und gegen körperliche Verletzungen und Traumata; die Maskerade als
übersteigerter Ausdruck eines mexikanischen Bewusstseins, das sich
in der Legende des Isthmus niederschlägt. Natürlich stellen Maskeraden

in gewisser Weise immer einen theatralischen Akt dar. Kahlo inszeniert
sich selbst durch ihre Kleidung. Auf der einen Seite ist darin einfach
die Identifikation mit dem Anderen zur Schau gestellt, wie es mit jeder
exotischen Kleidung einhergeht, seien es Hippie-Straßenmode oder
Designerkleidung von Zandra Rhodes. Auf der anderen Seite werden
darin Kahlos traumatische Erlebnisse der Vergewaltigung und Zwangs-
sterilisation dramatisch verdichtet. Dies wiederum verbindet eine körperliche mit einer symbolischen Versehrtheit, die wir aus psychoanalytischer
Perspektive mit dem Begriff der Weiblichkeit in Verbindung bringen
können. Zugleich vermitteln die unerschrockene Zurschaustellung und
die Meisterschaft der Kleidung Stolz und Selbstvertrauen. Dies kann
wiederrum mit der traditionellen Vorstellung der Tehuana-Frau als mäch-
tige und starke Frau in Verbindung gebracht werden, mit Tehuantapec
als Ort eines mythischen Matriarchats. Wie in Plaths symbolischem Verständnis von Weiblichkeit kann auch in Tehuantapec die Frau als Symbol
für Macht und Stärke verstanden werden. In zwei zentralen Gemälden
ist das Kleid auf einem Kleiderbügel und vom Körper losgelöst, als eigener
Bedeutungsträger, dargestellt.

Diese Augen

Kahlos Ikonografie ist präzise gestaltet und enthält über die Kleidung
hinaus weitere wichtige Motive. Ihr Haar wird zur Metapher, ob kurz
geschnitten oder wallend, geschmückt mit Bändern, Kämmen, Blumen
oder Schmetterlingen. Auf einigen Gemälden ist ihre Oberlippenbe-
haarung zu sehen, auf anderen wird sie weggelassen. Sie neigt dazu, ihre
Augenbrauen als starke, durchgehende Linie zu betonen, während dieses
markante Detail auf Fotografien viel weniger ausgeprägt oder gar
nicht vorhanden ist. Ihre Selbstporträts haben immer einen kraftvollen
und gerichteten Blick, der den Betrachter oder die Betrachterin direkt
adressiert.
„Sehen Sie sich diese Augen an“, soll Picasso an Rivera geschrieben
haben, „weder Sie noch ich sind zu so etwas in der Lage“. Apokryph oder
nicht, es scheint angemessen, Kahlos Konzentration auf die Augen in
ihren Gemälden mit derjenigen von Picasso zu vergleichen. Sie ziehen
den Betrachter sofort in ihren Bann, durchdringend und mit absoluter
Selbstsicherheit. Schließlich sind da noch weitere Ausstattungsstücke –
insbesondere die Wunden und die Affen. Die Wunden sprechen für sich.

Dort, wo sie am deutlichsten und blutigsten zu sehen sind – wie in der
Serie nach ihrer Fehlgeburt in Detroit: *Henry Ford Hospital* and *My
Birth* – oder an anderer Stelle, wie in *A Few Small Nips* oder dem Votiv-
bild *The Suicide of Dorothy Hale*, stehen sie in direktem Zusammenhang
mit den Themen Geburt und Tod als Gewaltakte. Die Affen – Nachahmer,
Grimassenschneider, Haustiere – werden mit Säuglingen assoziiert
(gewünscht, verloren, verstorben), mit Diego (als Affe, als Kind), mit Frida
selbst (mit Gesichtsbehaarung), mit Mexiko (mit seiner üppigen lokalen
Pflanzenwelt) und mit der tropischen Natur (im Gegensatz zum kalten
industriellen Norden). Erneut wird die scheinbare formale Einfachheit
von Kahlos Gemälden mit ihren traditionellen Bezugspunkten durch ihre
metaphorische und allegorische Komplexität widerlegt.

Kahlos Beziehung zur mexikanischen Bildsprache hat auch bei der
Rezeption ihres Werks im Ausland eine Rolle gespielt. Mexiko übt seit
langem eine große Anziehungskraft auf Künstler*innen und Intellektuelle
aus, denn es ist eine Art halbmythisches Land, ein Ort der Projektion
von Träumen und Fantasien: Majakowski, Eisenstein, Lawrence, Lowry,
Huston, Hart Crane, Edward Weston, Burroughs, Breton – die Liste lässt
sich fortführen. Vor allem Eisenstein machte sich die Legenden Mexikos
zu eigen – darunter die von Tehuantapec und dem *Sandunga* – und
versuchte, sie in seinem Film *¡Que viva México!* nachzuvollziehen. Der
Kahlo-Kult greift diese historische Faszination auf, eine Mythologie,
die zunächst in Mexiko selbst, während der „mexikanischen Renaissance"
der 1920er Jahre als Identitätsmythos konstruiert und dann anderswo
oder von Besuchern als Mythos des Andersseins reinterpretiert wurde.
Diese Mythologie Mexikos ist die eines alternativen Amerikas, das
im Gegensatz und in Opposition zum Norden, zu den Vereinigten Staaten,
gestaltet wird. Natur versus Manufaktur, Traum versus Realitätsprinzip,
Magie und Wunder versus Wissenschaft und Technologie, Menschlichkeit
versus Mechanisierung, Vergnügen versus Arbeit oder Unterdrückung,
Akzeptanz versus Verleugnung von Tod. Diese Antinomien strukturieren
auch Kahlos Werk – ebenso wie die visionäre Vorstellung einer Ver-
schmelzung von beidem, wie sie und Rivera sie metaphorisch in den
Landwirtschaftsexperimenten von Luther Burbank verwirklicht sahen.
Die Verfügbarkeit dieses Mythos – und seine mögliche Anziehungskraft,
wie bei allen Mythen des Andersseins – bietet eine Grundlage für
Fridamania.

Von einem puristischen Standpunkt aus betrachtet, mag der Kult um
Kahlo sie als bedeutende Künstlerin disqualifizieren. Aber das trifft auf
Kahlo genauso wenig zu wie auf Plath. Wenn wir uns für einen Moment
der Literatur statt der bildenden Kunst zuwenden, fällt auf, dass die
Literaturkritik gegenüber Werken mit mythischem Status sehr gespalten
ist. Melvilles Großer Weißer Wal wird akzeptiert, ja sogar bewundert,
Mary Shelleys Frankenstein-Monster schon weniger, und Bram Stokers
Dracula findet kaum Anerkennung. Und was ist mit J. M. Barries Peter
Pan oder Wodehouses Jeeves? In der Kunstgeschichte tauchen diese Fragen
kaum auf – mythische, ikonische Figuren gehören ins Kino oder in
Cartoons, nicht in die Kunst. Lediglich in der Pop Art, wenn Lichtenstein
oder Warhol Werke schaffen, die sich parasitär zur Populärkunst ver-
halten, wird diese volkstümliche Mythologie zugelassen, und auch dann
wird angenommen, dass die hohe Kunst als Metadiskurs ihren Gegenstand irgendwie aufwertet, indem sie ihn sich aneignet. Der Mythos ist
etwas anderes als der Kult, aber die beiden sind eng miteinander verbunden. Kultfiguren greifen fast immer auf Mythen zurück, so wie es auch
Kultfilme tun: *Casablanca, Rebel Without A Cause, Blade Runner.* Im Fall
von Kahlo ist das Entstehen einer Fridamania zum Teil auf ihre Auseinandersetzung mit mythischem und psychoanalytischem Stoff zurück-
zuführen, aber gleichzeitig ist Kahlos Kunst ohne sie nicht denkbar.

Angesichts des kulturellen Status, den die Kunstwelt sich selbst
zuschreibt, könnte es sein, dass Kahlos Status als Künstlerin in dem Maß
abnimmt, in dem ihr Status als Kultfigur zunimmt. Dies ist nicht
zwangsläufig so, wie das Beispiel Van Goghs zeigt – obwohl Toulouse-
Lautrec hier wahrscheinlich der bessere Vergleich wäre. Ich glaube jedoch,
dass Kahlos Position als Künstlerin über den Moment hinaus, an dem
sich das modernistische Paradigma auflöst, gesichert sein wird. Ganz
gleich, ob wir Kahlo aus dem Blickwinkel der Frauenkunst, der Kunst der
„Dritten Welt" oder des Surrealismus betrachten, ob wir uns für die An-
eignung volkstümlicher Darstellungsformen oder den Übergang zwischen
marginaler und hoher Kunst interessieren, Kahlos Gemälde schauen
uns direkt ins Gesicht. Als Künstlerin ist Kahlo vergleichbar mit Tanning,
Carrington, Agar oder den bekannteren Surrealistinnen, die alle unterschätzt werden; und als Surrealistin *tout court* ist sie vergleichbar mit
Miró oder Matta oder Lam oder Masson. Die mexikanische Kunst muss
neu bewertet werden, ebenso wie die Stellung der beiden für sie überaus

wichtigen Künstlerinnen, Kahlo und María Izquierdo. Kahlos Verwendung
volkstümlicher Darstellungen ist komplex und einzigartig. Eine Neube-
wertung der Outsider-Kunst, die jene künstlichen Abgrenzungen überwin-
det, die um bestimmte Kunstformen, wie die Kunst der Psychotiker*innen
oder die naive Kunst gezogen wurden, kann ihr nur zugutekommen.
Wenn wir erst einmal erkannt haben, dass selbst ein Künstler wie Jackson
Pollock einen Außenseiteraspekt hat, wird es schwer sein, Kahlo dies
vorzuhalten. Dies könnte sich sogar als eine ihrer größten Stärken erweisen.

Paradoxerweise drohte ausgerechnet Kahlos Erfolg am meisten
Schaden anzurichten, weil er die Aufmerksamkeit von Künstlerinnen der
Sechziger- und Siebzigerjahre ablenkte, deren Ruf noch nicht gefestigt
war – so unterschiedliche Künstlerinnen wie Eva Hesse, Judy Chicago oder
Mary Kelly. Vor allem Kelly ist eine Künstlerin, deren autobiografisches
Werk dem von Kahlo auf seltsame Weise ähnelt, obwohl es formal voll-
kommen anders ist, intellektuell anspruchsvoller und nicht die unmittelbare Anziehungskraft hat, die Kahlo auszeichnet. Es ist wichtig, Kahlo
neben solche Künstlerinnen zu stellen, sie historisch zu rekontextualisieren,
um die Geschichte der Kunst von Frauen insgesamt neu zu bestimmen
und ihre Fundamente zu stärken. In ähnlicher Weise muss auch die mexikanische Renaissance wieder neu beleuchtet werden. Ich habe zu Beginn
erwähnt, dass ich mich für Kahlos Werk interessiere, weil es meiner Mei-
nung nach die orthodoxen Interpretationen und Doktrinen der Moderne
in Frage stellt. Seitdem ist die Umgestaltung der Moderne selbst an vielen
verschiedenen Orten und aus unterschiedlichen Gründen im Gange.
Frida Kahlo war ein guter Ausgangspunkt dafür. Aber wir müssen unsere
Neubetrachtung der Kunst des 20. Jahrhunderts noch ausweiten und
ergänzen, indem wir jeden Aspekt der Moderne betrachten, der margina-
lisiert worden ist, und die Rolle der Frauen, der nicht-westlichen
Künstler*innen und der Außenseiter*innen oder Exzentriker*innen neu
bewerten. Durch diese Arbeit werden wir die Wichtigkeit der Fridamania
relativieren und uns wieder auf die Komplexität, Intensität und ver-
blüffende Schönheit ihres Schaffens konzentrieren können.

Das vorliegende Heft ist aus einem Besuch von Laura Mulvey am Seminar für Filmwissenschaft der Universität Zürich im November 2022 hervorgegangen. Neben einem Abend und einem kleinen Ausstellungsdisplay im Cabaret Voltaire gehörten die Diskussion von *Crystal Gazing* (1982) im Kino Xenix und ein Workshop für Doktorierende zum Programm. Zwischen den Veranstaltungen zog sich Mulvey zurück ins Hotel, um an einem „secret essay" zu schreiben. Einige Wochen später stellte sich heraus, dass es sich um ihren Text über Chantal Akermans *Jeanne Dielman, 23 quai de commerce, Bruxelles* (1975) handelte, der am 1. Dezember überraschend von Sight & Sound als Gewinner der „Greatest Film of all Times"-Umfrage bekannt gegeben wurde.

Veranstaltung und Heft lassen einige Momente der letzten 50 Jahre Revue passieren: Mulveys kanonischer Essay zur „Visual Pleasure", als Vortrag 1973 gehalten, zwei Filme von 1982 – *Frida Kahlo / Tina Modotti* und *Crystal Gazing*, ein Essay von 2003, der unter dem Begriff „Fridamania" das Verhältnis von Weiblichkeit, Pop und Gesellschaft mit Blick auf die künstlerische Moderne analysiert, die Kanonisierung von Akermans Film im Jahr 2022. Was ist aus diesen Daten heraus-, was ist in sie hineinzulesen?

Mulveys Vortrag im Cabaret Voltaire folgt dem Modus der Rückschau. Er reflektiert die historischen Bedingungen, die 40 Jahre zuvor ihr und Peter Wollens Interesse an Frida Kahlo und Tina Modotti geweckt haben, und zeichnet den Kontext ihrer gemeinsamen kuratorischen Arbeit nach. Neben der wissenschaftlichen und filmischen Arbeit der beiden ist es diese weniger bekannte Seite Mulveys und Wollens, der wir mit diesem Heft Aufmerksamkeit zukommen lassen wollen.

Aus der binären Gegenüberstellung von Kahlo / Modotti, die der Film und die Ausstellung in den 1980er Jahren zum Strukturprinzip nahmen, wird dabei 2024 ein loses Quartett – Mulvey / Wollen / Kahlo / Modotti –, das die vielfältigen Arbeitsschritte von Bergung, kuratorischer Arbeit, Ausstellung, Verfilmung, Rezeption und Reflektion neu anordnet und aktualisiert. Dies mit Laura Mulveys Hilfe, die sich mit uns auf diese Rückschau eingelassen hat – wofür wir ihr herzlich danken.

Pascal Maslon, Volker Pantenburg, Caroline Schöbi und Linda Waack
für das Harun Farocki Institut
Zürich, Februar 2024

Impressum

Herausgeber*innen: Pascal Maslon, Volker Pantenburg, Caroline Schöbi und
Linda Waack
Redaktion: Pascal Maslon
Übersetzungen: Caroline Schöbi / Linda Waack (Wollen), Pascal Maslon / Volker
Pantenburg (Mulvey)
Gestaltung: Daniela Burger, buerodb.de; Assistenz: Alix Stria
Lithografie: prints-professional, Berlin

Druck: Druckerei Sportflieger, Berlin
Fonts: Neutral BP, Excelsior
Papier: Munken Lynx, Efalin Feinleinen
Auflage: 1000
ISBN: 978-3-00-078431-6

Dank an: Antje Ehmann, Anna Faroqhi, Lara Faroqhi
sowie Laura Mulvey, Salome Hohl (Cabaret Voltaire), Oliver Fuke, Nicolas
Helm-Grovas, Andrey Lazarev (Whitechapel Gallery), Rob Lucas (New Left Review)

Abbildungen:
S. 2, 14, 15: Cabaret Voltaire, 8.11.2022, © Romain Mader
S. 16: Ausstellungsansicht Whitechapel Gallery, Frida Kahlo / Tina Modotti, 26.3.
bis 2.5.1982, © Whitechapel Gallery

© 2024, die Autor*innen und Harun Farocki Institut, Berlin
Veröffentlicht von Harun Farocki Institut

www.harun-farocki-institut.org
HaFI 021

HaFl 021 wurde mit Mitteln des Farocki Forums am Seminar für Filmwissenschaft der Universität Zürich produziert.